Ernie Frantz's Ten Commandments of Powerlifting

2nd Edition

"Godfather of Powerlifting"

Published by: SUCCESS by DESIGN Publishing
Lombard, Illinois 60148
E-mail: info@motordoc.com
http://www.motordoc.com

This publication is designed to provide accurate and authoritative information in regard to the subject matter covered. It is sold with the understanding that the use of the information contained within does not imply or infer warranty or guaranties in any form. The author and publisher highly recommend that entering the sport discussed herein requires good physical condition as determined by a medical authority and be done under the guidance of an experienced and certified trainer. The sport of powerlifting is considered an "extreme sport," and inexperience or physical defects can cause irreparable harm to the veteran or novice athlete. While this book represents guidance for the beginner or experienced lifter, it, in no way, represents medical or direct training direction.

ISBN-13: 978-0-9712450-8-2

TABLE OF CONTENTS

Foreword—Publisher   vii

Foreword—Ernie Frantz   xi

Man of Iron (Autobiography)   1
    Update 2013   8
    The World of Powerlifting . . .   14
        Powerlifting   14

The Big Three   17
    The Squat   17
    The Bench Press   25
    The Dead Lift   29

Frantz's Ten Commandments   32
    Frantz's First Commandment   33
    Frantz's Second Commandment   35
    Frantz's Third Commandment   37
    Frantz's Fourth Commandment   38
    Frantz's Fifth Commandment   40
    Frantz's Sixth Commandment   41
    Frantz's Seventh Commandment   43
    Frantz's Eighth Commandment   45
    Frantz's Ninth Commandment   46
    Frantz's Tenth Commandment   48

All-or-None Concept	57
Psychological Blocks	59
Cycles and Goals	63
The Frantz Routine	67
Monday	67
Squat	67
Deadlift	68
Bench	68
Tuesday	68
Squat	68
Deadlift	68
Wednesday	69
Thursday	69
Squat	69
Deadlift	69
Bench	69
Friday	70
Saturday	70
Squat	70
Deadlift	70
Bench	71
Supplements	73
The Diet	76
Protein Guide	79
Rest and Relaxation	87
Spotting for Safety	89
Training Partners	91
Injuries and Rehabilitations	93
Women's Powerlifting	98
Common Complaints	102
Sore Joints	102
Stretch Marks	103
Constant Feeling of Fatigue	103

Powerlifting Myths   105
   Powerlifters Are Dumb   105
   Muscle Turns to Fat   106
   Powerlifters Are Muscle-Bound   107

Official Rules for the Big Three   109
   Squat   109
      Causes for Disqualification of the Squat   110
   Bench Press   110
      Causes for Disqualification of the Bench Press 110
   Deadlift   111
      Causes for Disqualification of the Deadlift   111

Powerlifting Now and in the Future   112

The Frantz Health Studio   116

Blaise Boscaccy (1984)   118

Bill Nichols (1984)   121

Francis Rudy Ruettiger (1984)   124

Maris Anne Sternberg (1984)   127

The Frantz Family in 1984   130

Powerlifting Glossary   135

FOREWORD—PUBLISHER

I rejoined the world of powerlifting with my first competition in October 2011 following a 15-year break due to a serious injury falling from a roof. In the 1980s and early 1990s, powerlifting was at its twentieth-century peak. The sport was open to new lifters, but the spotlight was on the "big boys," the heavy squat attempts, the giants, the big benches and the big deadlifts. Throughout the world, powerlifting has remained a significant sport as well as a practice and training for sports of all types.

Powerlifting is the art of moving weight quickly in the form of three major lifts: squat, bench, and deadlift. Each of these lifts, using proper form, involves the whole body as well as mental fortitude. If you are not using both, the power of the mind as well as power of the body, you will not be able to move the superhuman weights observed at many local and World events. It is now not unusual to see squat attempts approaching—or exceeding—1,000 pounds, or bench attempts over 500 pounds, or deadlifts exceeding 600 pounds. It is not without its dangers—as I am writing this I am recovering from a serious training accident that occurred away from my team on substandard equipment (I broke one of the commandments).

At the time of the publication of this book, there are multiple federations globally with a variety of rules associated with the lifts and judging. There is also controversy surrounding raw versus single ply- versus multiply-geared lifters. The number of raw first-time lifters has escalated and often exceeds the number of geared lifters at many meets as virtually anyone can enter the sport and compete at any level of experience. Additionally, social networking has generated the ability to broadcast whole meets live, athletes can record and upload their attempts, and advice can be shared between lifters worldwide, even when they don't share the same language.

While there is virtually no money in the sport, with very few financially sponsored lifters, there is the thrill of no restrictions from entering a meet. I have observed 60-plus- and 70-plus-year-old men and women make their way up to the bench or squat rack and knock out weight that your average young gym rat would be impressed by. Engineers, doctors, business leaders, truck drivers, fast-food employees, therapists—you name it—all participate and speak the same language of powerlifting, and lifters who persist enjoy a brother- and sisterhood that extend worldwide.

I met Ernie Frantz, after having heard about him for decades, during an Illinois local meet. He had suffered some business losses related to the loss of his gym in Aurora, Illinois, due to fire. He was selling off damaged items and continuing his support of the sport. When we met, he was proudly wearing his "Godfather of Powerlifting" T-shirt and kept me listening with rapt attention to stories related to his early years of strength sports and powerlifting. He continues to train lifters and visit gyms, providing advice generously.

After about a year of meeting Ernie off and on at competitions and gyms, we realized that a wealth of information would be lost to time once Ernie would no longer be able to continue. When I attempted to obtain a copy of the original *Ten Commandments* book, published in 1983—not only could you not find a copy, but those who had obtained them held on to them tightly—not willing to part at any cost. I did obtain a copy from Ernie in order to work this project—the development of the second edition. It was decided that a few items (amounting to about five paragraphs) would be removed, spelling and grammar corrections made, new pictures (actually, some of the original, plus new) would have to be obtained, but that the lion's share of the original book would remain unchanged. Why? Simply because it remains one of the most complete books on entering the sport and maintaining the athlete—easy for the beginner and a great reference for the elite lifter.

We are also working on a second project—Ernie Frantz's biography. It is a collection of stories and experiences that bring to light a generous spirit and full life bringing the sport to where it is today. Intrigue, excitement, adventure, and rubbing shoulders with local and world leaders. When I first heard some of the stories I was taken aback. Then, as we sifted through the evidence, pictures, and news stories, we believe that the biography will expose our chosen sport well for the general public, once again.

And so, please enjoy this second edition of the original *Ten Commandments—* the advice and wisdom of one of the giants in sports, let alone, powerlifting . . .

Howard W. Penrose, Ph.D., CMRP
President, SUCCESS by DESIGN Publishing
and 2XLPowerlifting.com
Lombard, Illinois
2013

FOREWORD—ERNIE FRANTZ

I wrote this book because I have something to contribute to the sport of power-lifting. I do not plan to waste your time, and I certainly do not want to waste my own. This book covers it all. It contains most of what I had learned in over 2 decades of powerlifting when I wrote the first edition in 1984.

Over the years, I have seen many men publish their "secrets." I have no secrets. What I do have is a successful way in which you can further (or start) your powerlifting career. I will not tell you to do anything that I have not done with success in the past.

I have trained many champions. All of them achieved their success through the use of my TEN COMMANDMENTS. I stress the basics because so many lifters forget them in clutch situations. People are not machines. The only way in which a human can master a set of instructions is to do them and do them and do them . . .

This book was written for future champions. The gender of the reader is not important. What is important is a spirit and drive to advance oneself. If your goal is power, I suggest you read on.

MAN OF IRON
(AUTOBIOGRAPHY)

As far back as I can remember, I have always dreamed of being strong. I used to idolize characters like Superman. They seemed like they had life under control. There was a certain confidence that they had that I longed to possess. I did not realize it at the time, but I would spend many years in search of this confident feeling.

I was born on the northwest side of Chicago on May 19, 1934. My father was employed as a housepainter and decorator. Mother was always the busy home-maker. I was the third addition to a very loving and warm family.

When I was young I never liked school. It seemed like such a big waste of valu-able time. I was popular with my classmates because I was a scrappy kid. I always stood up for my rights, and the other kids followed my lead. This quality occasion-ally got me into trouble, but mostly being the leader gave me the power to choose. At the time, I chose to ignore education.

I come from a Catholic background, but at times did not act like a Catholic. I do believe in God; yet, I am lax in some of the practices. All through childhood, I felt unsatisfied with what life had to offer. I knew there was a special spot in life waiting for me to find it, but there were so many places to look that I grew confused. I needed someone or something to give me direction.

Before I knew it, I was in a different spot somewhere in Korea. I had been sent there to stop a war. My only goal at that point in life was survival. I spent nearly a year fighting on the front. A person never really values anything until they might lose it. War taught me to value my life and my precious time on earth.

While in Korea, I had a great deal of time to reflect on my short life. I prom-ised myself I would set goals and try to make something out of the rest of my days. God must have been on my side; I safely escaped from Korea and was honorably discharged from military service. My military career forced me to always stay posi-tive. A negative attitude while in a battle can lead to hasty actions. Positive thinking would be the key to many future successes.

The year 1953 marked the start of my now-successful career in iron. I weighed a whole 132 pounds and originally bench-pressed a measly 135. That is right—I started my training barely able to bench my body weight. Back then, there was no such thing as powerlifting, so I body built.

The first few years were spent doing thousands of calisthenics. I did push-ups and sit-ups until I was blue in the face. Gradually, I inserted free weights into my routine. I was still being driven by the desire for power that I felt as a child. I wanted desperately to build a physique I could be proud of.

Suddenly, I was not only developing a body but also a hunger for education. I enrolled at Southern Illinois University to study law enforcement. Eventually, I was to spend close to 5 years of my life engaged as a police officer. I even worked my way from sergeant to chief of police in a local town.

Slowly but surely, my physique was developing into a prizewinner. I started to enter local contests and won many trophies for "best body parts." As I gained a little contest know-how, I started to pull in award after award. Weights were helping to shape my identity. I was feeling great and starting to look like a champion.

By this time, the law and I went our separate ways. I found myself back in school. This time around, my main course was carpentry. I was healthy and wanted to start to use my newfound strength to build things. Thanks to weight training, I was overflowing with ideas, and I was starting to gain that certain confidence.

I get a lot of satisfaction out of constructing objects with only my wits and my bare hands. I eventually became a skilled carpenter. I even worked as a building contractor for a couple of years. I was making houses, but I still felt there was something missing in my world.

I had already been married twice. Life just did not seem like it was dealing me a fair hand, so I started to look for something special. It did not take long before I found it. Her name is Diane, and she has been the source of my happiness ever since the first day we laid eyes on each other.

In the year 1962, I made a major decision that would affect the rest of my life. I opened the Frantz Health Spa. My physique was turning into a showcase, and it was all because of weights. I decided to open up a gym and pass my knowledge on to other people who could use it to better themselves. I felt I had found my spot in life.

I continued to further my education. I took extensive courses in all sorts of fields. More important, I was starting to learn from the biggest school of all. I was learning from experience. I found myself setting goals and striving to meet them.

In 1967, I took second in the Mr. USA contest. All my training was starting to pay off. People were telling me how far I could go in championship bodybuilding. However, I was not listening; I was preoccupied with a new aspect to my old sport.

The mid-'60s found me engaged in powerlifting. I always liked to work with heavy iron throughout my bodybuilding routines. When I found out there were contests that tested a man's strength, I decided to devote most of my workout to the development of power. My childhood dream of strength was about to materialize.

I started to work the big three religiously. Soon, I developed routines and schedules to boost my big lifts. I fell in love with the squat and developed a passion for the deadlift. I sat down and wrote out my powerlifting goals. My first and biggest goal was to be a champion. I decided to dedicate the rest of my life to fulfilling that dream.

I began to win a lot of local meets. My lifts were getting bigger and bigger. So was my weight which had risen to a sturdy 181 pounds. I was on my way to being that champion. There were still a lot of workouts between me and my goal, but I was headed in the right direction.

Meanwhile, the Frantz Health Studio was doing great. My enthusiasm for powerlifting was contagious. My gym was always full of men building good physiques, and now, all of a sudden, it was full of a new breed of lifter. This new breed had only one goal . . . and that was power. A lot of my good bodybuilders decided to quit pumping and give power a try.

Then it dawned on me. Instead of the whole gym having to travel to a contest, why couldn't I hold my own powerlifting meets? There was a lot of talent in my gym and people came from miles away just to compete against my lifters. Eventually, running a meet would make me a profit, but those first few years were spent just spending money to bring the best together for all-out competition. I did not mind spending the money to support the competitions. I considered it an investment in the future of the sport.

I was quickly gaining experience in the new sport of powerlifting. People were constantly coming to me for advice. Everyone had questions, and I tried my best to answer them, but there was a lot I did not know. I kept working out harder and heavier. I was determined to test the limits of human strength.

I started to learn about the body's ups and downs. I was learning the secret of the cycle. Knowledge was coming at me so quickly that I was soon rising above the average powerlifter. I was slowly reaching the status of an elite lifter.

As I learned more about powerlifting, I passed it on to the men at my gym. My role as a coach was getting bigger and more complicated. I had the makings of the best power team in the country, but I lacked experience in the sport myself. My team and I were growing together. The Frantz Health Spa was growing too. Soon, the establishment overflowed its original floor and spread to the entire building. Three floors devoted to the pursuit of physical superiority!

In 1971, I made another one of those decisions that affect the rest of one's life. I decided to go to prison. No! I was not a resident. I went to prison to teach the joys of physical exertion to the less fortunate in this world.

I was hired to construct a weight program for the kids at Valley View Youth Center. It was a great job, but at times, a sad one. Some of those kids were just there because they lacked guidance. They never had any real direction or positive force in their lives.

I showed them progressive weight routines that would strengthen their bodies and add to their confidence. My thinking was that a strong body would lead to a strong mind. I knew once they had reached some lifting goals that they would want to reach for, and set, other goals in life. If nothing else, I tried to give them the desire to better themselves.

In 1974, I graduated to the adult division of the Illinois Department of Corrections. My job, again, consisted of setting up weight lifting programs for both the inmates and the staff. I built good power teams at Sheridan and Statesville and currently have a good team at the Joliet Correction Center.

Prison is a strange world. It is full of men who have been caught making mistakes. Some of the men were just led astray in life; others were full of hostility for a world they feel is unfair to them. I try to get the men to display this hostility constructively in the gym. I show them how to do the exercises, and then hope they adopt them into their way of doing time. I feel powerlifting can change a person's way of thinking about himself and the world around him.

I have trained a lot of very good lifters in prison. Some of them never touched a weight after their release from confinement. A few of them have left prison to join my gym team. To me, prison is the ideal place to teach strength training. In prison, you have very little to distract you and only one goal: that of survival. The opportunity for concentration is tremendous.

My career as a coach is a happy one. I have had the good fortune of training at least 30 lifters to the top. I have worked with some really gifted people. Each one of them has taught me something. I would not trade my life as a coach for anything. There would be no sense to knowledge unless you could pass it on.

Sometimes a man will try to impress me with his strength. He will try to buy a favorable impression from me by showing me how strong he is. I do not mind people who are proud of themselves, but I do get annoyed when one lifter will try to impress me by sacrificing another one's total. Some men have natural strength, and others have to work for every ounce of power they have. I have never bragged or boasted, and I do not flaunt success. This is the attitude I try to convey to all of my team members.

In 1974, I put it all together. I was literally on top of the world. This was the time in my life when my dreams would be reached. I was training hard, and so I decided to enter both the major powerlifting events and also the top bodybuilding tournaments. Everybody thought I was out of my mind. They kept telling me I could not retain all of my strength if I cut up to enter physique shows. My mind was made up. I weighed 181 pounds of pure muscle. I had been training for nearly 2 decades and felt it was time I took on the impossible.

I breezed through the 1974 Nationals, turning heads and setting records. Slowly, people started to take me seriously. I was scheduled to take on the best in powerlifting at the Worlds. I was also scheduled to enter the Mr. USA Physique Contest. The only problem was they both fell on the same day! Fate had dealt me a difficult challenge, but I was determined to meet it and come out on top!

The contests were only 12 miles from each other. I made up my mind. I would enter both events and try my best. It was a decision that would either bring me glory or certain defeat. I felt that after years of hard, heavy workouts, that glory was worth gambling for.

The powerlifting Worlds was my first challenge. I warmed up trying to conserve my strength. Then I erupted to a record-breaking first place in the 181 class. Everybody was real proud of me and telling me what a great day I had . . . but the day was not over for me.

I ran over to the Mr. USA contest with winning on my mind. I felt drained, but driven. I was being driven to prove my own faith in my physique. I was on top of the world, but I felt I could go further. This physique show would be my statement to the universe.

I spent 6 hours under hot lights, flexing for all I was worth. I put everything I had into that show. At the end, I was awarded second place. I felt content with my accomplishment. I had bested a lot of good career physique men and stunned the world of weights with my double victory.

I had done it! For 1 day in 1974, I was the strongest man in the world, and I had the second-best physique in the country. That was the answer to all my prayers. As a child, I had wanted strength; as an adult, I possessed power.

The Frantz Health Spa continued to do well. I even opened up a store within the gym. I stocked it with anything that a weight lifter could benefit from. Then I started a mail order business. The store was a huge success and the fastest-selling products were my own inventions.

By this time, I had gained a lot of expertise in the field of powerlifting. The Frantz Ten Commandments were becoming a way of life, but I was concerned about the need for better equipment. I started to use my ideas by applying them to my own products. I was determined to make powerlifting a safer sport.

I developed a protein powder that was designed for extra energy and excellent muscle recuperation. I then manufactured my own lifting suit and knee wraps. I designed both for extra support in heavy lifting. I felt that most suits back then just could not hold up when the squat got over 600 pounds.

I am living proof of my products' success. I use them in all facets of my lifting. I was blessed with a good business. My products were purchased in all states and three countries. I feel I have contributed to the growth of powerlifting as a sport.

I have held over 50 World records. I still hold many of them to this day. I have won tons of local meets and my share of National and World contests. I felt my life was a success and I had reached my goals, and then . . .

My wife Diane decided she wanted to be a powerlifter too. At first, I balked at the idea. Diane had been doing some bodybuilding using free weights in her routine, but powerlifting was another story. She proved her desire by training harder than any other novice I have ever coached.

Diane was determined to be a female powerlifter, and I was bound to help her. I put her on a program with heavy emphasis on the squat and deadlift. Right before my eyes, her strength started to grow. I had nothing to compare her gains with, so I decided to make her the standard for women's powerlifting.

Diane's presence in the gym attracted other females. All of a sudden, I had a novice powerlifting team full of women. A whole new area of coaching was opened up to me. I eventually molded a few of these eager women into very good lifters.

My wife has since set World records in both the 123- and 132-pound classes. She has won lots of trophies and has earned a lot of respect in the powerlifting world. Diane recently won the 1984 Women's Nationals. As an award for my work with some of this country's top female powerlifters, I was named one of two coaches for the USA 1984 Women's National Team while competing at the Women's Worlds. I am very proud of this distinction.

At the time I wrote the first edition of this book, I was over 50 years of age, and yet, I did not think I had peaked as a powerlifter. My body weight was 200 pounds. I was a lot heavier than my original 132-pound frame; yet again, I was also a lot stronger.

My best lifts in practice in 1984 were: squat 840 pounds, bench 515 pounds, and deadlift 820 pounds (with straps). Most people think age would have slowed me down and sapped my strength, but, in fact, the opposite is true. I feel maturity is giving me an edge over most of the young, raw powerlifters of today.

My goal was to win the Worlds again. You may think that sounds unrealistic, but I barely lost the 1983 Nationals (by 5 pounds), and at the time I was 49 years of age. I knew I could post a 2,000 pound total in the 198-pound class.

My life is one filled with goals and aspirations. Besides winning the Worlds, I also wanted to accomplish two more things in the near future. One was to open a gym equipped to handle the rehabilitation from any injury. I think it is important to have the proper equipment on hand for people who have to start the road to physical conditioning all over again. The other major goal I had was to host my own version of the Worlds. I would like to be able to use my training at smaller power meets to bring the best in the world together for an all-out confrontation of power.

I still workout heavy 3 or 4 days out of the week. Time is not aging me—it is making me stronger. I try to lift as heavy as I can, as often as I can. I keep pouring it on and increasing those poundages because to me, power is part of my life. I will never retire from the sport that has brought me so much success.

If you are not as physically fit as you feel you should be, I advise you to start your own strength career. If you are weak, do not waste time thinking about it; start getting in shape. Build a foundation by doing calisthenics to give you confidence, and then start powerlifting.

The key is to remember to always think positive and to strive to better your previous accomplishments. You will have to make some sacrifices. The big one will be giving of your time to better yourself. You will have to give both your body and your brain lots of workouts before you will be able to claim victory, but the work is worth it.

In my old age, I find a lot of little kids look up to me. I do not mind being idolized—it reminds me of when I used to be a Superman fan. Times have not changed much. I still admire the man of steel, only now, I am the man of iron.

UPDATE 2013

In powerlifting, just as in most professions and sports, there are legends that exemplify the sport, the icons such as Ed Coan, Louie Simmons, Mike Bridges, Dave Tate, and many more, then there are the legions of Internet self-proclaimed experts, scam-coaches, and others. Through all of this, the true artists are eternal. They are viewed as legends because they consistently perform as do the athletes they train.

Ernie Frantz has affected the sport of powerlifting more than anyone, alive or dead. He has been a World Champion, inventor, or originator of many of the key gear and equipment used today, founded one of the world's largest powerlifting federations, and is the trainer of champions.

Some of Ernie Frantz's lifters include: Ed Coan, Bill Nichols, Noel Levario, Jose Garcia, Jason Patrick (all 1,000-plus squatters), Ray Makiejus, and Joe Atef, and legendary female lifters such as his wife Diane Frantz, Nancy Dangerfield, Sidney Thoms, Stephanie van DeWeghe, and many others over the past 30-plus years.

Following the original publishing of the Ten Commandments, Ernie made the decision to split from his joint bodybuilding and powerlifting accomplishments and focus solely on the sport of powerlifting. He continued to grow the sport and, through his consistent generosity, support a great many lifters.

Following hardships occurring as a result of a fire that swept through his gym and business on Broadway Avenue, Aurora, Illinois, on November 28, 2011, the Frantz Power Team dispersed to several other gyms. While we have been working on this project, Ernie has plans to reopen the gym and pull the team back together.

Back in the good old days, my time was spent doing a lot of impressive body work. I would spend all day pumping a muscle through exercise, and then participate in feats of strength. I was young and wanted to experience everything there was to feel. I had no real power goals: I just lived for the moment. Now I realize the value of thought and planning during any body movement. I still do feats of strength, only now, I use my head as well as my body.

By the 1960s, my body and my mind were both developing at a rapid pace. I had some definite goals in mind, and I truly wanted to see them materialize. At this point, I knew that iron was part of my life.

My friends and family were starting to get behind me in my dream to be the best. By 1965, I was beginning to feel that I could be the best. After that, I started to act like the best, and before I knew it, I was winning.

It took a lot of hard work to build a physique I could be proud of. I have always been my strictest critic, but I have never fostered a negative attitude. When I felt I had room for improvement, I simply tried to improve.

The idea is not only to build a good physique, but to maintain it. I work heavy because I want muscle that will stay with me for the rest of my life. I believe to get the biggest muscle, you have to properly lift the heaviest weight. My personality is partly due to my weight lifting, and my social life has always revolved around my power routines. If I ever stop pushing the weight, I'll stop breathing. I enjoy power-lifting because I can see and feel the results. Every time I enter the gym, I have a goal in mind and a strategy to meet it. Powerlifting allows me to exercise my self-control as well my body.

When I started to work at the Valley View Youth Center, I hoped to contribute some of my knowledge to the young and undeveloped. I really enjoy showing a person how to develop their physical and mental power. I think if everybody lifted weights, this world would be a better place to live. A person who pushes themselves to the limit is a person who will always strive to better themselves, both in and out of the gym.

In the early 1970s, I started to build powerlifting teams within the adult division of the Illinois Department of Corrections. Above is my most successful team, and I am proud of each and every member. They may not look pretty, but they all were dedicated lifters.

From these pictures, the makings for this book were built. Since the opening of these doors in the early 1960s, I would estimate that literally thousands of people have found the key to unlock a better life. The gym has grown, and with it, has the bodies of many men and women. I hope to expand the gym even more and bring an even greater training facility to more people. I want to get the whole world to lift weights because weights are fun.

THE WORLD OF POWERLIFTING ...

Powerlifting

Powerlifting is the most exiting sport in the whole world. There is no other sport that combines as much raw energy and technique as it takes to become a good powerlifter. When a man walks out to the platform, it is he against all odds. There is no excuse for personal failure. A man has control of his whole life in the seconds it takes to lift the weight. I like to be in control of my life, so I powerlift.

I have tried to participate in other sports, but nothing brings out the best in me like strength training. Powerlifting is a world filled with hard work and sudden excitement. The thrill of lifting a big weight after training for so long is a thrill you won't soon forget. I cherish the moments of triumph I have had because I know the amount of hard training that went into making them possible. I am proud of my powerlifting accomplishments, and I would not trade them for the world.

I have seen many people take up powerlifting as a hobby and have turned it into a habit. It really is something else to watch an ordinary human being when he or she realizes they possess power. A novice (beginner) will usually have a lot of desire, but not much technique. As the workouts start to accumulate, the total begins to climb and the lifter's enthusiasm begins to grow.

At first, your total will move up quickly, but eventually, you will peak and be forced to struggle for your gains. The sudden spurt is attributed to the fact that you are awakening muscles you never knew you had. Once these muscles are awake, the gains will start to come more slowly. The slow gains are always the most rewarding. Your initial gains are chalked up as a universal happening. Everyone has a great beginning, but the future is what you have to work for. The future is also what separates the good powerlifter from the elites. Lifters must prove themselves over time before they can be classified in the sport of powerlifting.

If people say they have only been lifting for a year or two, I try to impress upon them the hard road ahead. I have proved my staying power by remaining in the iron game for the past 6 decades. Powerlifting is a fun sport when the gains are coming regularly, but can be a real nightmare when you go into a lifting rut. I try to convince people not to take themselves too seriously because their power careers should be a rewarding experience, but sometimes a lifter will feel pressured into making gains.

The individual who expects to see gains in his power total every week of every year is asking too much of himself and the sport. The body can only take so much shock before it shuts itself down for repair. You cannot rush a good thing. Powerlifting, like life, takes some practice before you can master it. I try to get novice lifters to understand that exertion can be fun and that if they train hard, the gains will come.

Your training should be one of your top priorities. You cannot expect to be the best unless you want to. A person has to want to train before they can get anything positive out of lifting. If you would rather be out drinking or running around, you might as well go ahead and leave the gym because you will not make any progress with that attitude. A lifter has to want to give the sport their all; you cannot force a person to try their best.

I treat the sport with a lot of respect because it deserves it. Weights have given me so much and asked very little of me in return. All the science of exertion requires is a lot of your time. You have to devote gym time and personal time into this activity. How good your gym periods are will be affected by how much of your personal time you apply to powerlifting.

The key to success is to apply yourself to your dream at all times of the day and night. On my way to the top, I kept a mental picture of my destination. I knew where I was headed and what it would take to get there. Believe me, it is perfectly normal to pursue a goal in this manner. Powerlifting is a positive sport because it takes up so much of your time. That may sound strange, but it is true.

Powerlifting allows you to set goals, and then go about doing them. This system of planning your moves to reach your desires can help you in all other parts of your lift. Weights can also give you the confidence and energy to meet all of life's challenges. Increasing your power can lead to a lot of other positive changes.

There are three different lifts that make up the sport of powerlifting. The squat opens the contest and is also my favorite lift. The squat is where you have the weight on your back and you crouch down and come up. Next comes the bench press; this is where you press the weight off your chest. The deadlift is the lift that signals the end of the contest and the posting of the totals. To deadlift, you pick the weight up off the floor and simply stand erect with it.

During a powerlifting meet, you have three tries at each lift. You can warm up off to the side, and then tell the judges your opener. From there, you will have two more tries to better your first attempt. You should always open light so you won't have to worry about making your attempt. For your second jump, you must add at least 10 pounds; for your third try, you can jump 5 pounds if you choose to.

If you miss a lift and follow yourself because no one else is at the weight that you want to try again, you have 3 minutes to prepare yourself. You can buy time by raising your attempt, but if you miss a lighter weight, it is difficult to come back and make a heavier one. A little-known trick for getting extra time when you miss your opener is to skip your second lift and tell the judges' table that you are preparing for your third attempt. If you do this, then you are allowed 8 minutes in which to prepare. You have to sacrifice one of your attempts, but it may keep you in the contest.

Once you post your openers at the judges' table, they sort them into a lifting order. They will then announce who is to lift, who is "on deck," and who is "in the hole." On deck means that you will be the next lifter. In the hole means you will be on deck next. Once your name is called over the loudspeaker as the lifter, you have 1 minute to get the bar in motion.

When you are called on deck, it is a good idea to prepare for your attempt. The lifter before you will be done before you know it, so use the extra time to get ready. If you prepare early, then you will not have to be rushed during that precious minute. I have seen lifters wait until they are called over the loudspeaker before they start to wrap, and before I knew it, they were squatting wrapless.

Powerlifting is a fun sport because you can see progress with your own eyes, both yours and your competition's. When you lift a weight you never before attempted, the feeling is like no other feeling. You get a content sensation that says, "I bettered myself." This feeling of success will stay with you for the rest of your life. Powerlifting is a healthy sport and one filled with personal achievements.

In powerlifting, additional body size comes as a reward for good training. Weights can cause you to grow muscle where you never thought you had muscle. There is no finer sport than powerlifting. It takes out your frustrations and leaves you with success. I would never have stayed in power if it were not for its amazing returns. I could have spent my life doing other things, but I chose powerlifting, and it is a decision I have never regretted.

This book is the result of all of my past successes and the attempt that led me to the victory platform. I hope everybody will read this book and give the words in it a try. It never hurts to try to advance yourself, and with the techniques in my book, there are no limits to your potential. The Ten Commandments were meant to be the handbook for the serious weight student. I hope everyone will give this book some thought and hopefully apply themselves to its teachings.

THE BIG THREE

THE SQUAT

This lift opens every meet. A strong squat can put you ahead in a contest and on your way to victory. The squat is an easy lift to master; all you have to do is learn technique and drive.

The first thing you must have is good equipment. A strong, snug suit is a prerequisite to a big lift. I manufactured my own suits. They were made of the finest material and designed for ultimate support. I used the Frantz sit-and-knee wraps when attempting any heavy squat. You can squat without a suit, but you'll not have that tight feeling you need for success.

Historically, I have always been a great squatter. In the 1970s and 1980s, I have been able to easily handle upward of 600 pounds at a body weight of 181 pounds. I have held and hold a lot of squat records. Squatting has always been a big priority with me. I like to start all contests with a big squat.

What time and practice has taught me is: Patience is a must. The squat, more than any other exercise, taxes the whole body. The weight on one's back reminds you of the urgent need to squat or rack. Your body and your mind have to work together for success. When you enter the gym to squat, you must give your training all of your concentration. You cannot expect to hit a big squat without investing a lot of mind control.

When you approach the bar, grip it with gusto. Lower yourself under the bar and position it on your back. Ride the bar high on your traps, but at least an inch below the top of your shoulder. Through repetition, the position of the bar on your back will feel normal. The key is to safely place the weight on your back with as little pressure on your spine and neck as possible. Eventually, you will develop a habit of always putting the bar in the same spot, but for now, be careful.

Now, slowly back out of the rack. Keep your feet a little wider, then shoulder-length apart, and point your toes outward (not forward, but at outward angles). Tense your body completely; every muscle should be contracted. By keeping your muscles flexed, you will prepare your body to not only squat, but to be on guard for any emergency.

Make sure you keep your head up. With your head tilted back, you will remain straighter and, thus, prevent excessive pressure on your spine. Most of the power for the squat should come from the powerful quadriceps in the legs. Try not to alter your stance throughout the movement. Many squatters develop the bad habit of dropping their head as they start to squat. This will not only throw off your concentration, but it may lead to injury.

We're ready to proceed. Break slowly at the knees. Keep your shins straight, but sit backward as if you are about to recline in a chair. When the lower part of your hips pass your knees, rocket upward. Remember, every muscle is tight. As you are coming out of the squat, push your knees outward. This movement will stop your legs from buckling in on you. The squat can only be dangerous if you lose control of the weight. Forcing your knees out will save you from most squat injuries.

When you start to squat, do not be afraid to let yourself go. It does not make much sense to get all wrapped and suited, and then go and cut your attempt. Make sure you get that hit. Good spotters will add to your confidence. If you have capable spotters, you have no excuse for not hitting the pocket. Find people you can trust, and then do your thing. If you are consistently stopping short of the pocket, get mad at yourself. The only way to fail is to first try. The only one to blame for a cut squat is yourself.

As you start your squat, lower yourself with control, then when you know you are in, start to come up. The motion should resemble a jack-in-the-box. Start out slowly, and then when you get to your bottom, blast out. This technique took me a long time to master, but it is worth the time. By flowing through the movement, the weight does not seem as heavy as when you stop at the bottom.

A lot of lifters go on a search and destroy mission. They will hesitate on the way down and actually search for the pocket. All this will do is destroy their lift. A style with hesitation will hinder your progress; you should learn to flow through your squat and not stop and search at the bottom. It sounds harder than it is; after a while, it will feel natural. If you are a novice, start out with this style now, and then you will have an edge in the competition.

That is all there is to it. Just remember to: grip, place the bar, step, plant, squat, and drive. These instructions sound easy, and they are, but most lifters never develop their squat to its potential. Some develop fears; others don't test themselves properly. You have to constantly push your squat upward by testing yourself and building confidence.

The body can adjust to any pressure. When a person puts 500 pounds on his back, he may fail, but if placed there often enough, the body will adjust. Most lifters are too easily satisfied and do not realize how much they can actually squat. I squat heavy at least twice a week. I keep the pressure on my body and continue to overload it, so that it will be ready for heavier and heavier poundages. You cannot expect to make good gains on no practice. Try not to neglect your squat. It is essential to keep the body used to heavy pressure. If you take frequent squat layoffs, you will spend most of your time squatting weights you have already squatted with success in the past.

That is the purpose to quarter squats in the power rack. Every time you overload the body it heals stronger and stronger. I have used up to 1,000 pounds in the rack. The idea is to force the body to accept the stress. I often stand with a heavy weight and just give my mind time to accept the fact that it is there. If my mind can hold a picture of me standing with 1,000 pounds long enough to squat 800, then the rack work was more than worth it.

Rack work not only forces the body to accept a lot of stress, but it allows the mind to get psychologically ready to perform a big squat. I will start out doing quarter squats in the standing position, and after loading on the plates, I will end up doing 2-inch squats off the safety bars. Rack work always gives me a positive feeling about myself and my lifting. I try to make gains in my quarter squats just as if they were full squats.

Whenever you are in the power rack, always keep the reps low if you are using heavy weights. Weights that are so heavy that they force your body to work should never be abused. Repetitions of five and under are advisable, but singles can do the job just as well. The idea is to overload the body with pressure; do not wind yourself by doing a lot of reps when one can do the job as well as 10 can.

Another little-known exercise that can be performed on the power rack is "bottoms." Bottoms are simply half squats performed from the bottom of the squat to the middle. Pick a weight you know you can squat with ease and go down into a full squat with it. Stop at the bottom, and then proceed to start upward. When you get halfway up to the standing position, stop and start down again. Repeat this movement for as many reps as possible. I usually do seven reps per set.

Bottoms will help you develop that flow-through motion we discussed earlier. They will also strengthen the legs in this part of the squat. Going down with a weight is easy; coming up is always the hard part. Bottoms will give you practice and much-needed experience at hitting the pocket and flying upward. Increase the poundages you use on your bottoms so you can continue to apply pressure as your muscles grow in strength.

I try to do rack work at least once a month. I usually use the rack on a Tuesday, and then take Wednesday off to recuperate. Recently, I have been ignoring the power rack, but plan to use it often as I prepare for this year's Nationals. The rack can be used to spice up an old routine and is a must for any beginner.

Sometimes, I will do a moderately heavy set of squats at the end of my routine. During this set, I will try to squeeze out as many repetitions as possible, and on the final rep or two, I will "pause" at the bottom. By stopping at the very bottom of my squat, I am forcing all of the leg muscles to contract, and as I start to come up, I am using all leg power. The reason I am using all my leg strength to do these reps is because I have taken away the momentum (downward motion) that causes me to flow through my usual squat.

Another movement I use to add variety to my workout is the "down set." I will pick a heavy weight (usually 5 pounds over my maximum poundage) and just do the downward part of the squat with it. I will rely on my spotters to bring me up out of the pocket and help me rack the weight. Needless to say, you must have good spotters before you can attempt any down set.

The purpose for this negative squat is to let the body feel the weight and to convince your mind that this new max is obtainable. I will usually attempt to make this squat cleanly during my next workout. What you are actually doing is setting yourself up to meet a new high by intentionally not trying it during your current workout.

I have told you a lot of extra tidbits to use in your squat routine. They are: quarter squats, bottoms, pauses, and the down set. I do not expect you to use them all in any one particular workout. I have mentioned them so you will have an added advantage over your competition. You can use any one of these methods to help you get new maxes, but do not overdo it. Your training may need an occasional boost, so keep these movements in mind. If you attempt to use them too frequently or in combinations, be on the lookout for signs of fatigue.

You should alternate these exercises and use each one to its advantage. Watch your squat and identify your weakness. If you need help on the bottom, do bottoms, or if the weight feels heavy before you squat, do the powerful quarter squats. These four movements will strengthen your squat and put you on the road to success, but they must be respected and used with care.

Breathing is important in any exercise, but it is most significant in the squat. Once you are ready to squat, I recommend that you take one deep breath, and then start your descent. Some lifters take several breaths and do not stop before they start to lower themselves. Too many gasps for air will only cause you to hyperventilate, and you must be ready to concentrate on squatting. That means you cannot be inhaling all that air and squatting at the same time. Try to limit your oxygen intake to one deep breath.

Another area where squatters differ on is the use of a safety belt. Some lifters say they will not use a safety belt until they get to their maximum attempt, but I disagree with this school of thought. A belt is a piece of equipment and should be used to a lifter's benefit. I use a belt when attempting any squat. Occasionally, I will warm up without a belt so I can better listen to signals coming from my body, but remember, I usually warm up with 145 pounds. Even with that light a weight, I still prefer to use a belt.

The reason some lifters give for going beltless is that it helps to better strengthen their lower back muscles. I would not know about that because I do not want to sacrifice my safety to find out. I endorse the use of the safety belt and hope that all novice lifters begin their career using one.

Bodybuilders will often state that full squats will give you knee injuries, so they use the parallel squat only. Most bodybuilders say this out of ignorance; some say it to justify their inability to master this movement. The full squat cannot automatically damage your knees, and I am living proof of that. Knee damage comes from performing the lift in an unprofessional manner. You are reading this section to learn how to do this movement properly.

Any movement performed through its full motion will develop the muscle to its fullest. As long as you squat without a lot of jerky motions, you will develop big, strong legs and never experience serious knee problems.

Sometimes I will use other exercises to strengthen my legs and, thus, help my squat. If I need some variety in my routine, I will occasionally employ the leg press or leg extension machine. These exercises will attack the muscle from a new angle, but remember: the only way to raise the squat is by working it.

You cannot expect the squat to soar if you spend your workout on your back doing leg presses. You have to stand under that weight and practice the good, old-fashioned squat before you can realistically expect to get good at it. Leg presses and the like have some basic benefits, but do not get attached to them.

When performing presses or extensions, try to keep your reps low and work with heavy weight. As a powerlifter, you have no need for light, quick sets. You want to mentally be prepared to handle maximum poundages. A lot of light sets will only throw off your body's timing. While doing these other leg exercises, pause between each repetition and make each rep count. The contest judges will not be interested in the amount of leg extensions you can do. The idea is to expand those leg muscles and keep that squat heading upward.

There you have it—everything you need to know about the squat. I have done my job; now, it is time for you to do your part—practice.

Jose Garcia

Jose Garcia

Ed Coan

Steve Goggins

Maris Sternberg

THE BENCH PRESS

First off, let me destroy a myth: Benching is not supposed to be fun. So many times I have heard lifters say, "The bench is my favorite because it is comfortable." The bench is a place where subtotals are made. If you want comfort, be a spectator. The only enjoyment I get is watching massive poundages leave my chest during big contests. When you approach the bench, do it with confidence. Walk up to it with a goal in mind. Then proceed to assume the position. Never walk up to a bench and just flop yourself down.

You should start your grip at shoulder-width. The closer your hand spacing is, the more triceps you will have to use. The further your grip, the more minor chest and shoulders you will have to apply. I suggest you vary your grip according to your strong points. Start out with a medium-width grip, and then alter it as you recognize your strong points.

I use a big arch. The arch will give your chest spring action. When you set the weight into your chest and hear the signal, the bar tends to explode upward. To arch, grab the bar with your hands and push your shoulders toward your feet. Your buttocks should remain stationary by clamping your knees to the bench. Your feet should remain firmly on the floor. Now just keep inching your body downward with your shoulders. The result will be an arch in your back.

At first, you will experience some discomfort. Like I stated before, our goal is power, not comfort. The more practice you apply to your arch, the more normal it will feel. Eventually, you will find yourself seeking a bigger and bigger arch. Do not worry about your height. The taller you are, the bigger the arch will be. A big arch and a wide grip will offset a tall frame and long arms.

Now we are on the bench. Next, we have to accept the weight. I always use a breathing signal to my spotter. When I breathe in, he hands me the bar. I do this because I feel a person cannot concentrate if he is talking to his spotters. You also cannot get a good breath if you are talking. The bench cannot be performed without oxygen. After you receive the weight from the spotter, you can exhale and get new air before you start the lift.

Now we are ready to attempt the lift. Lower the bar slowly (with control). It is important that you keep your elbows tucked in toward the sides of your body. This will give you plenty of triceps power when the time comes. So many times you see strong lifters usually trying to heave poundages with their arms away from their bodies. Your chest can lift lots more than your arms can push, so practice keeping your arms tucked in.

The scene is set. We are ready to make those records. We hear the judge's signal. The first move I make is to contract the buttocks. Tense your hip area in. This will not bring you off the bench, but it will start that momentum your chest will need to drive with. At first, you will not have any timing, but with practice, you will learn to contract, and then drive as a reflex action. If you are a novice lifter, I suggest you start your career with this movement in mind.

Now, keep your arms tucked in and push. Give it everything you have. When the weight gets moving, start to drive backward toward the rack. This will allow your triceps to step in and better help your chest. Make sure you do not start backward too quickly. If you do, the weight might stall in a bad spot—namely over your face.

That is all there is to it. All you have to remember is: clamp, arch, breathe, elbows, control, contract, and drive. Seven things to practice until they become habit. You would be surprised at the amount of lifters who do not have a bench system. With my pattern in mind, anyone can become a great bencher. All it takes is time and desire. You must practice with an eye on your form. If you do not monitor your style, you will never develop a consistent technique.

I perform a few auxiliary exercises. I do heavy (weighted) dips. These help my lockout when I get to heavy poundages on the bench. Dips give my triceps the shock they need to push through a rough bench. I usually do five sets of five reps, but I may alter these numbers to fit my needs and my mood.

I also advocate the use of negatives on the bench. I prefer to use 10 or 20 pounds over my max at the time. I slowly lower this weight to my chest for three repetitions. As I let the weight down with control, my spotters bring it back up, and I repeat the process. I try to keep the heavy pressure on my chest. By slowly lowering the weight I can handle, I develop my chest and my confidence.

When doing a negative on the bench, always use three spotters for added safety. Another important tidbit to remember is to fight the weight all the way down to your chest. A lot of lifters will look real good on the first part of their negative, but will let the weight drop to their chest when it gets 3 or 4 inches from its destination. The reason for this is because the top part of the negative is usually supported with a lot more triceps power; the closer you get to the chest the more effort it takes to control the weight.

I would rather see a lifter save some energy to fight that second half of the negative, instead of wasting it on a good top half and no second half. The idea is to work the chest, so choose a weight that will feel heavy, yet still be controllable. Negatives will only work for you if you work at them.

Some champions use a tremendous amount of weight and lower it with little control for one rep. I personally feel that a few pounds over your max for three reps are more than enough. The pressure on your body for that long a period will make your normal max as light as a feather. I used to use awesome amounts on my negatives. All I got from them was an inflated ego and sore shoulders. The important thing is to work the chest and not destroy the shoulders.

Another bench strengthener is my system of "shorts." I do shorts to improve my explosion off my chest. If you can heave the bar off your chest, you can give your triceps a chance to step in and complete the lift. Shorts will perfect the starting motion of your bench and make your chances for success a lot better.

I usually do two sets of shorts, but beware—these sets will leave you winded, so do them at the end of your bench routine. My first set will consist of 10 short reps; my second set with a light weight will consist of 20 short reps.

A short is simply a half repetition, but the key is it's the bottom half. Choose a weight you can handle for a long period of time. At first, choose a weight between 50 to 100 pounds under your max. After awhile, you will find your perfect poundages. Now, lower the bar to your chest and have a spotter place his hand from 6 to 10 inches over your chest. Try to touch his hand with the bar 10 times.

To accomplish this feat, you can arch up (your buttocks, if need be, can come off the bench), but make sure you do it with as much speed as possible. It is the quickness that will eventually help your explosion during a strict bench. Next, choose a lighter weight and try to do 20 shorts.

If you cannot squeeze out every rep, use a lighter weight during your next short workout. Trying to use heavy weight is the principle, but not if you have to sacrifice proper execution. The exercise will not work unless it is done right. As an added test, after you have done a short set, lower the bar back to your chest and try to do a full repetition. This will be a real drain on your already worked chest. Make sure your spotters know of your intentions, so they can be ready to assist you.

Negatives and shorts will help the bench tremendously, but eventually, you may want to work your chest from a different angle. That is where dumbbell presses come in. A heavy dumbbell press will shock the chest and allow you to work the muscle from a broader angle.

Dumbbells will allow you to lower the weight further than you could with a straight bar. Therefore, you can work the muscle more thoroughly. Again, I stress the need for low reps and constant tension. Just because you are holding dumbbells does not mean you should forget your power goals.

I have suffered numerous shoulder tears over the last 30 years. I ask you to learn from my experience. Do not get cocky on the bench. The idea is to develop your chest and increase your power. Do not let your ego dictate your jumps on your actions.

I would be a 600-pound bencher if I avoided the dreaded shoulder tear, but unfortunately, I haven't. Always pay attention to what you are lifting at all times. There is no excuse for a stupid injury. Once you tear a shoulder, you will heal, but your bench may suffer for the rest of your power career.

After 6 decades of benching, I have learned a lot of things. The most important is to bench in practice as you would in competition. By benching strict now, you will develop your chest and arms to their fullest. So many lifters advocate cheat benches (bounce benches) as a method for handling heavier iron. I used to bounce a lot, but have found it to be an inferior substitute for the strict bench.

Strictness will develop your muscles—bouncing will shock, strain, and perhaps, tear them. There is no sense in attempting to do a lift you have little control over. You must respect iron. Bouncing a weight off your chest makes no sense when you will eventually have to do it strict in a contest.

There you have it—everything you need to know about the bench. I have done my job; now it is time to do your part—practice.

THE DEADLIFT

Richard Zenzen

This is the lift that ends all contests. A strong deadlift is extremely important. It will not only give you the victory, but it will psychologically destroy your competition. It is not right to be the strongest lifter in a contest and to lose your hold on first place because of a poor deadlift.

I deadlift in a flat slipper. Experience has taught me that to deadlift, one must have both feet firmly on the ground when tugging. Any elevation tends to draw me off balance and consequently, take away from my base of power. I stand before the bar and try to imagine myself as putting my feet through the floor as I pull.

In the 1980s, I developed the Frantz Rocker. This style of deadlifting has proven to be quite effective when handling heavy poundages. The Frantz Rocker is the result of years of experimentation with every deadlift form you can imagine. If you can picture it, I have, at one time or another, tried it.

I approach the weight and stand with my shins touching the bar. My feet are about 6 to 8 inches apart. The toes are pointed straight-ahead. I feel with the feet firmly pointed forward that more of your powerful leg muscles can be used. The idea is to start your pull by employing the strong leg muscles your squat is developing.

Your grip should be on the outside of your legs (2 to 4 inches from the leg). If your grip is too wide or too narrow, you will have trouble pulling your shoulders back; therefore, your grip should allow you to pull your shoulders back before the lift begins. A lot of lifters will wait until they are at the lockout part of their deadlift before they pull their shoulders back, but I prefer to start my motion with the shoulders already locked out. In a competition, you will have to pull your shoulders back for the lift to count.

Next, keep your head up and rock forward, then quickly go back into a full squat and blast upward. Your momentum will practically lift the weight by itself. All you have to do is keep your shoulders back, head up, and drag the bar across your shins up your thighs. When you first try this movement, you may fall backward or forward, but do not let that stop you from trying it again.

Throughout the movement, your arms should remain locked out. No one can curl the amount of weight they can deadlift. If your arms bend during the rock forward or squat back, it will throw your timing off. Keep those arms straight! If you find it hard to keep your arms straight, you should increase the depth of your squat motion backward. You may be going too deep and losing your balance.

Most people fear the deadlift because they think it is a cause for severe back pains. This is true only if the deadlift is done improperly. With the Frantz Rocker, most of the power comes through momentum and leg strength, not through the back muscles. Nothing will ruin a deadlift faster than a bad attitude. If you think the deadlift will hurt you, it will, because you will never develop a good one.

If you choose to do reps with your deadlift, I suggest you start each repetition as a separate single. Often, lifters will pick a weight up off the floor and bounce or bank out six or seven reps. I disagree with this method. If you train your body to bounce a deadlift, the rep will more than likely be with poor form and all back. When it comes time for the big lift, your body may revert back to that same poor form. Can you picture yourself in a competition trying to explain to the judges that you have to bounce the weight before you start your deadlift? They may tell you to go play basketball!

I advocate the use of heavy singles. I cannot see the purpose of doing a lot of repetitions with the same weight. I would rather do a good heavy single, and then add more weight to the bar. In this way, my body can get used to the style and experience heavier poundages at the same time. If I know I can deadlift 500 pounds, why should I do it more than once when I am anxious to try for a new maximum output?

If I want to feel a weight I have never done before, I will do a negative. Negatives, in this sense, are reverse deadlifts. I will assume the position, but I will have other lifters pick the weight up off the floor. One on each end, they will bring it up for me. It will be my job to lower the weight down to the floor with control. Sometimes I will lower the bar back down to the top of my knees, and then drag it back up my thighs. This will help me with my lockout.

Usually, I lower the bar with as much control as I can muster for particular poundage. When the bar gets about 2 inches from the floor, I stop it and count to five. This will assure me that I can handle the weight. When I actually try the lift and it starts to leave the floor, instinct will take over and the positive feeling I had during the negative will power me through the movement. For most people, the hardest part of the deadlift is the beginning. Once the weight is off the floor, most people are content with pulling, but the problem is usually getting started.

Many people develop mental blocks about the deadlift. The only way to overcome them is through hard work. I suggest a lot of negatives and a lot of practice sessions. The deadlift can, at times, be a mental nightmare.

You can do assistance exercises to strengthen the back. A few good ones are the bent-over row and the shrug, but these exercises will not win a contest for you. Eventually, you will have to master the deadlift. I have found that the way to get a strong deadlift is to practice it until you can do it sleepwalking. Deadlift so many times that it becomes second nature to go out on that platform and pull.

If you have never deadlifted before, do not feel badly. You may be very lucky because you have not had the chance to develop the bad habits that stop so many lifters from being excellent deadlifters. You cannot only start your career today, but you can start it with a strategy. The Frantz Rocker can lead you to the powerlifting career you want so badly.

There you have it—everything you need to know about the deadlift. I have done my job, and now it is time to do your part—practice. NOTE: for more conversation on the deadlift, turn to the Eighth Commandment.

FRANTZ'S TEN COMMANDMENTS

Ernie Frantz and Ed Coan with 1,440 lbs

Equipment (wraps, suits, etc.) should be a benefit, so learn to use it wisely.

Make sure you warm up properly and listen to your body.

Act like your light lifts are heavy, so your heavy lifts will feel light.

Concentration separates the good from the best.

Keep every body part tight during the entire movement.

When trying a new style, work up slowly, but work hard.

There is no excuse for a lack of practice.

A good deadlifter will always finish strong.

Bodybuilding and powerlifting do not mix. Make your choice—beautiful muscles or raw power.

Work with a positive attitude. A winner thinks he can, and a loser never thinks.

FRANTZ'S FIRST COMMANDMENT

"Equipment (wraps, suits, etc.) should be a benefit, so learn to use it wisely."

Over the years I have heard so many people complain about equipment. Most felt that it hampered their ability. I fully advocate the use of suits, wraps, belts, and any other instrument that will make lifting safer. Powerlifting is not a sport for daredevils, so safety should always be the top priority.

In a contest between human and iron elements, of course, the iron will win out. The only time the person has a chance to be successful is if they mentally and physically prepare for the confrontation. Equipment allows you to get the edge you need to be successful. A sculptor against the rock is an uneven match until you give the sculptor at chisel.

Before I squat heavy, I make sure my suit is tight. I also wrap my knees and very firmly so they will not be vulnerable to the pressure on my back. My wraps will not only give my knees an elastic feeling, they will also give me a confident feeling for success. If I were to try to squat my max without wraps, my knees would shake and divert my attention from my concentration.

When you have equipment—use it. A loose suit in the squat makes no sense. Take every precaution to ensure your safety. Being lazy is a poor excuse for an injured person. Powerlifting is a serious sport and should be treated as such.

I have seen champions and many contests misuse or abuse their equipment. I treat my gear with respect and try to keep it in mint condition. A worthless piece of equipment is just that—worthless.

When first warming up for an event, I will wear my equipment a little loose. This way, I can better gauge my body's mood. If I feel tired and have a lack of enthusiasm, I will wrap earlier in my squat routine; if I feel good, I may wait to wrap. On the average, I usually wrap and suit up for my last four sets of squats. It all depends on what my body tells me.

The wrists are very a fragile part of the body. The bands I wear are constructed to keep the wrists tight and protected from excessive overload during the bench. Wrist wraps give me added insurance when I'm trying to push to my limits.

The body is usually injured when it takes the shock of the weight unexpectedly. Wraps of any kind keep the tightness in the area. This warm, tight feeling makes that body part less likely a target for sprains and strains. An injury will usually occur when the lifter least expects it to, so I try to keep this tight feeling whenever I lift any weight.

Some people argue that equipment makes you dependent on artificial means to lift the weight. This makes no sense. If a person wears gloves in the wintertime to keep his hands warm, the gloves are not the instrument that later manipulates objects. We wear gloves to keep our hands ready for action. The powerlifter uses his equipment to prepare his body to lift the weight. Powerlifting is not a survival of the fittest contest. The object of the sport is to safely and cleanly lift the weight to the desired position.

I am not dependent on my equipment, but it is part of me. I use it to get my body ready for the lift. If a person gets to a point where they have to use it or they cannot lift, say 50 percent of their max, then I would say they are psychologically dependent on their equipment for strength. The idea is to use equipment and not to let equipment use you. If you're getting dependent, cut back and do more sets without it, but make sure they are light sets. There is no sense in risking an injury just to prove a point to yourself or anybody else.

Do not be afraid to modify equipment to fit your needs. Over the years, I have made numerous changes to several items. That is why I produced my own equipment. I took all the ideas I have had over the years and applied them in an effort to make powerlifting an even safer sport.

I have been at meets where I've seen men squat without wraps or deadlift in heels. I do not think most people choose to lift this way. I feel they have to because they do not know any other way. I advise you to watch other lifters as they prepare to lift. Study their movements and the method in which they handle their equipment. You may see something you could use in your routine.

Beware of a few things that could be disastrous to your powerlifting career. If you see a lifter smiling while he wraps his knees, be careful—he is not pulling hard enough. A good wrap will cause you to grunt heavily. Also, a lifter shouldn't feel comfortable standing around in their equipment. If they do, then the equipment is not tight enough. A lifter should not be able to walk comfortably with the squat suit up. If he can, then he is not getting his money's worth out of the suit.

I can tell you how to use equipment, but you will learn more through the actual use of it. Try to draw mental pictures from the following paragraphs. When

I wrap my knees, I start the wrap about 2 inches under my knee and wrap upward. I wind the bandage around my leg, and then crisscross the knee. I never try to wrap higher than 4 inches above my knee. I like to actually cross my knee on at least three different passes. I pull on the wrap as hard as I can, as often as I can. The tighter the wrap, the more elastic my knees will feel during the actual performance of the squat.

As for your squat suit, it should be a real struggle to put on. The material should dig into your body. A good suit will eventually make your legs go numb. A partner should pull your suit up for you, and it should fit extremely snug. In fact, you should not be able to crouch down with your suit up and no weight on your back. Powerlifting suits occasionally need adjustments.

The powerlifting belt should be worn as tightly as you can tolerate it. I usually ask for assistance in tightening the belt. A training partner will tug on the belt until I latch it.

As you can tell from the above discussion, when I say tight, I mean *tight*. The idea is to feel secure while attempting to lift any weight. Through the educated use of equipment, you can achieve higher totals and thus, move ever closer to becoming a champion.

FRANTZ'S SECOND COMMANDMENT

"Make sure you warm up properly and listen to your body."

When attempting to lift the weight you have never lifted before, you should be ready. Being ready means taking the time to properly shock the body to accept the new pressure. Jumping under a big weight can be a serious mistake that you should never make. There is a right way and a wrong way to attempt heavy loads.

I warm up using a ridiculously light weight. While doing this lift, I will look for cramps or areas of my body that may be sore. I will flush blood throughout the muscles I am going to use. It is not uncommon for me to start the day squatting 145 pounds and end with 750 or so. I am no hurry to reach my max. When I get there, I will be ready to handle it and the speed in which I reach it will be a safe one.

I feel taking the time to properly warm up has been the key to my link in my power career. I am not embarrassed to start the bench at 135, or an empty bar, when people expect me to load on the plates. The idea is to post the big totals when it counts. If people want to watch me bench heavy, that is fine. They will just have to wait until I get there.

I start my deadlift a little heavier. The reason for this is because I usually deadlift after a squat; thus, I am already warmed up to a certain extent. Also, when using the Frantz Rocker, light weight has tendency to throw me off balance (backward).

If I can take the time to warm up, I certainly hope you will. Lifting heavy weights is important, but safety is the main thing. You can be the strongest man in the world, but if you have an injury, you may not be able to enjoy your status. I not only plan to outlift my competition, I also plan to outlive them.

I have seen 500-pound squatters feel they are too strong to use light weights, hurting themselves trying to warm up at 350.

Don't let this happen to you. Put your brain to work at defeating your ego. A couple of sets are all it takes to assure you in your body that you are ready to get heavy.

No matter how strong you get, remind yourself of the importance of proper warm-ups. Likewise, while warming up, your body may give signs of excessive fatigue. Take the science seriously. If you're feeling weaker, cramped, work a little more on light sets before attempting to lift heavy. Your body may tell you not to attempt any maximum poundage on that day. If it does, then don't. Just make sure that you do not develop a habit of ducking your max. The better you get at judging your mood for the day, the better you will get at powerlifting.

If you stay in tune with your body, you cannot go wrong. It is your body that will eventually make you a champion. If at all possible, perform a few calisthenics before you begin your workout. Stretch those muscles and be on the lookout for problem areas. Do some imaginary squats and see how the motion feels. It will be to your advantage to find a cramp for you apply any weight on it. Remember to listen to your body, and your career will be happy one.

Powerlifting is a safe sport *if* you take the necessary precautions. Spend some time warming up those muscles and learn to understand the language of your body. The bigger you get, the more you should be careful. It makes no sense to spend your years working hard, and then sacrifice it all in one second of bad judgment. Being a champion is a long-term investment. We cannot expect to be the top overnight. A person has to spend some time going through the ranks. If you pay close attention to your training, you can continue your climb to the top safely, and more important, swiftly.

To save precious gym time, you can start warming up on the way to your workout. As you are headed to the gym, start to shake out your limbs. Get the blood circulating throughout your body. Start pumping those muscles using nothing but your desire to have a good workout once you arrive at the gym.

I hope you take these words seriously. Warming up can add years to your power career and provide you with many happy moments. People are not machines that can just turn on and off. Lifters should gradually work their way toward their power goals. A little extra time to make a lot of difference.

FRANTZ'S THIRD COMMANDMENT

"Act like your light lifts are heavy, so your heavy lifts will feel light."

Throughout my career, I have pretended my light lifts were heavy, so my heavy lifts would feel light. The idea is to get the body ready for the big one by using perfect form on all the little ones. Every set you take is aimed at making your maximum lift a successful one. If you fly through your warm-ups, you will probably stall on your big lift. Try to remember: the only way to make the big lift is to prepare for it.

When I take a light set, I take it with as much care and motion as a heavy one. For instance, when I am squatting with 400 pounds, I will use the same style and go to the pocket just as I would with a heavy set. This way, when it comes time to squat with 800, my body is already in tune with the motion in-depth. It would be a real shock to your body if you cut all of your squats and asked your body to go deep in the pocket with your max on your back.

Often, you will see a lifter go through his warm-ups, only to miss during his final try. I feel it is mentally and physically beneficial to you to give your light sets your full attention so you can set yourself up for a good finish.

Physically, your body will be all warmed up and ready to go. Also, your body will be used to the stance in position for a big lift, thus, making it easier to do. In fact, the body will actually be driven by anticipation toward your big lift. Your body will want a new high as much as your mind will.

Mentally, your body will feel psyched and ready for the big one if all the other sets were done correctly. Making your easy sets look easy by using good form will give you a confident, assured feeling for success at a higher weight. The more confidence you have, the better the odds will be on you hitting that high. If you do not prepare yourself mentally for your heavy set, you will feel sluggish and not be able to get yourself together—and this will lead to failure.

I suggest you treat your light lifts with as much respect as your heavy ones. The only way to make your maximum attempt is to first complete your openers. It is important to make those new highs, but it is just as important to finish your workout safely. By acting like your light lifts are heavy, your heavy lifts will feel light, and you will guarantee yourself a long and happy power career.

Once you're warmed up and ready to climb to your max, never admit to yourself that the weight is heavy. The easiest way to psych yourself out is to tell yourself you cannot do it. When you get into the heavy part of your workout, pretend it's your light part. Look and feel confident and you will be amazed at the amount of strength you will show.

The secret to a successful lift is to physically and mentally complete the attempt before any negative vibrations can set in. Sometimes lifters will concentrate on their attempt while holding the weight; other lifters will think about how light the weight is before they touch it. You will have to decide which style is best for you.

If you can devote time to mental psyching while the weight is on your back, then do it, but some lifters will get their thoughts together before the attempt to do a lift. The deadlift is the place for you to see lifters who hesitate to prepare and other lifters who get it together and run up to the platform and pull.

Throughout the workout, you should be thinking, *Light lifts heavy, so heavy lifts will feel light.* A good lift only take seconds to complete, but the preparation for the attempt can take hours. You have to devote a great deal of time and energy into reaching your dreams, but when the white lights flash, it will all be worth it.

FRANTZ'S FOURTH COMMANDMENT

"Concentration separates the good from the best."

Concentration is one of the keys to success. If you want something bad enough, it must be worth thinking about. Nothing worth keeping will present itself unless you want it badly enough. You'll have to use your mind power to focus in on your goal.

I carefully plan out every move I make in a lift. I try to picture its successful completion so I can get that confident feeling that comes with planning. Some lifters will just attempt a lift and pray for the outcome. I tried to make the desired outcome a reality by thinking hard about it.

You would be surprised at how natural a lift can feel after you have thought it out. I picture myself doing a bench. I feel the motion and imagine the entire movement. When it comes time to actually do the lift, it seems like I have already done it. I try to picture myself in a lift that is at least 100 pounds over what I plan to attempt. If I can successfully see myself doing the inflated lift, the actual lift will feel as light as a feather.

Many people approach the bar with no brain activity. They do not know what they're going to do; all they know is they want to do it. Not me. I meet the bar with a definite energy. I tell myself, "Hey, you have done this before; do not sweat it." Then when I get the bar in motion, my instincts take over and the power does the rest. If you practice a lift both in your mind and with your body, the lift will feel as natural to you as anything else.

Do not let yourself get distracted by meaningless chatter. While lifting, try to block out all the noise and confusion. Just picture yourself doing the lift. Keep telling yourself that you could do twice the weight currently on the bar. Concentrate and everything else will follow in place. The trick is not to let anything stop you from doing your best. If the gym is noisy, so what? You are not there for peace and quiet—you are there for power. Getting distracted is an easy thing to do if you let yourself wander from your objective.

It may help for you to lift with some slogan in mind. For instance, you can repeat "I am power" over and over until the bar starts to move. And at my gym, we occasionally lift with music. The idea is to get the body in rhythm with the song. Some lifters use mirrors as a method for focusing their full attention on the lift, but be careful that you do not get addicted to using some artificial means of concentration.

I suggest you practice using different methods of concentration. The main thing is to keep your mind on what you are doing. You cannot control the environment, and do not let it control you. The best form of concentrating is to use good old-fashioned mind power. If you can master your brain, you will be on your way to doing many big things—both in powerlifting and in life.

Some lifters take courses or listen to lectures on such topics as yoga, meditation, or self-hypnosis. These studies can give you inspiration and ideas on how to improve your train of thought. Like anything else in life, you must think about concentrating before you can expect to be good at it.

Not thinking about an attempt is the poorest excuse for missing a lift. Often, you will see a novice lifter run out to the platform after just completing a discussion with fellow lifters on a trivial matter. A master lifter knows what they have to accomplish. They will not waste their brain waves in idle conversation when they know they have to do a heavy lift. A smart lifter will use his gym time to concentrate on gym activities.

The more thought you put into a lift, the more success you can expect. When I'm doing anything close to my max, I block out all noise completely. You can rant and rave all you want to because my attention is focused inward. People asked me afterward, "Did you hear my cheering?" All I can say is, "At that point in my life, all I heard was that 800 squat coming up."

The best time to practice your concentration is before the contest. At a meet the noise and confusion can at times seem unreal, so I advise you to get your thoughts together before you show up. An actor will experience stage shock. Well, powerlifters have their own version of this condition. A powerlifter will go through "platform panic." The best way to avoid this embarrassing situation is to be ready to lift under any conditions.

Do not get so emotionally attached to any particular bench or set of squat stands. Be mentally prepared to do your best on anyone's equipment. Be ready to squat off on milk crates if that's what it takes to win a trophy. I often recommend that a lifter open a contest with a lighter weight if they have never lifted off that equipment before. You don't want to give yourself a chance to get mentally psyched out.

Weight lifting is a sport for strong people, but wisdom plays an important role in deciding who wins. Get wise. Think about what you are about to do, and then try your best. The brain can be just as instrumental as the body in getting you to the top of this big sport.

One form of concentration I do not advocate is the use of physical punishment. Some coaches will slap their lifters to clear their heads and prepare for they attempt. I cannot see a purpose to inflicting pain on any lifter. If someone were to slap me, it would make me mad—I'd be ready for revenge but not ready for concentration. I've seen some big lifters bang their heads against solid surfaces before they lift. They claim this helps them to think.

I hope you find a method for success that does not involve the use of torture. Powerlifting is a sane sport—do your best to keep it that way. Concentration can be fun. So can powerlifting.

FRANTZ'S FIFTH COMMANDMENT

"Keep every body part tight during the entire movement."

If the body is tight you can accept any shock. If someone were to hit you in the stomach, it might hurt, but not if you tensed your stomach muscles first. This is the general idea behind keeping every body part tight. You're anticipating the weight before it comes, instead of being caught unaware of its pressure upon experiencing it.

As long as your body is tense and rigid, the risk of injury is small. Picture this: You go to squat, your legs are tight, but your arms are lightly clutching the bar. What will happen is the weight will feel heavy and will probably shift on you. Now, if you are holding on firmly with every muscle ready for action, you would probably make the lift with ease. The thing to remember is that the iron has no brain; therefore, you have the advantage if you are prepared to accept it.

Most lifters do not flex their legs during the bench; the lift is entirely one for the upper body. During the bench, I keep my whole body tense. I turn myself into a rubber band. I am ready to accept the weight and toss it back up. Now, if I were to just lie on the bench and flex my chest and arm muscles, half of my pushing power would be useless. Pay close attention to your stands the next time you are attempting to lift and you will see if you are guilty of a relaxed position.

By keeping every body part tight, I also give myself a confident feeling. I feel strong; therefore, I am strong. This tight feeling will aid my concentration. If I can "feel" my body as a rock ready to accept iron, my enthusiasm and confidence will shoot through the roof. The better my concentration, the more likely I will do well in my attempt.

I've seen some lifters lean to the extreme. You will see a man about to squat, and he will be shaking all over the place. I do not think we need to overexert ourselves to the point where it interferes with our confidence. A simple quick flex before you start the movement would be sufficient. All we are trying to do is prepare ourselves for the pressure.

If you look around the gym you will notice a lot of lifters flex their upper body far too much during the deadlift. The deadlift is primarily a leg and back movement, but some lifters, fearing the weight, will flex their upper body as if it will decrease strain. Needless to say, flexing the arms but not the legs will not pull a deadlift. During this lift you should make sure you flex your entire body with the same intensity. While using the Frantz Rocker, it helps to have those concepts ready for that initial movement.

When you have some spare time, practice flexing your whole body without the burden of any weight. Learn to master your muscles so that when you enter the gym, it feels natural to flex it during your weighted movements. At first, an entire flex of all your muscles will feel strange, and it may sap you of some strength, but keep on practicing and you will eventually be able to do it anytime and anywhere.

A lazy person may have some trouble exerting all of his energy to master this concept, but there is no need to worry because a lazy person has no future in powerlifting. Learning to flex your muscles can also benefit you in other aspects of your life. It really fills out a shirt, and it can add zest to your calisthenics. Take some time out of your life to master this tightness principle.

Staying tight can be beneficial to every aspect of your training. You can help your confidence, your warm-up, and ultimately, your maximum attempt. Practice staying tight during all of your lighter sets. Learn to master those muscles, so in the big sitcoms you are ready for it. The idea is to stay tight so you can get big and strong.

FRANTZ'S SIXTH COMMANDMENT

"When trying a new style, work up slowly, but work hard."

When the body is used to a movement, it is less likely to sustain an injury. If you squat every day with the same style, the muscles will be used to this movement. If you were to change your style, the shock may cause your body to reject the weight. As we all know, when the body rejects weight, an injury is a definite possibility. When a powerlifter is accustomed to heavy, hard work, it is often hard for them to successfully compete in more agile activities unless they warm up to them first.

For instance, if you bench 400 strict, your muscles will be used to lowering and raising 400 pounds. Now, if you were to walk into the gym and decide to bounce

420 pounds, an injury would likely happen. Your muscles would be trained for a certain pattern, then all of a sudden, you switch styles and rep. A change in style will also throw off all of your training in the area of concentration. A new movement will leave you bewildered and in trouble unless you prepare for it beforehand.

When I try a new style or different technique, I make sure the weight is a light one. I have seen a number of lifters get hurt by shifting their feet or changing their hand position while attempting to heave their biggest totals. If you have an idea that a new style may help you, I suggest you use it from the beginning of your workout.

Do not be afraid to unload some plates and start small. It is better to start small and work your way up, then to start with your max and not make it up at all. Powerlifting is not a speed game. You should always give your body and brain time to adjust to new movement before overloading them.

You cannot change horses in midstream. Do not expect to be able to switch your style and automatically surpass your previous total. Do not get me wrong, I had others take stances and successfully altered them, but I had them use a weight I knew they could handle with ease; thus, their confidence and comfort with the new movement were positive. I did not just change their stance and walk away. I stayed by their side and coached them through their first couple of new sets.

When selecting a change in position, use some discretion. First, try it on a light set, then work your way up again. This will assure you that the new style is definitely for you. A new style is not necessarily a good style. Some styles can be hazardous to your health. Take time out to choose wisely.

As a coach, I often alter lifters' stances to fit their needs. If you are tall, you may have to squat with a wide stance, short with a close one, but the main thing is to change them safely. I urge you to start light and work, instead of trying to prove something by getting a new max quickly. Do not let your ego take over for your common sense. Powerlifting is not a game of impressions. It is a sport of skill.

The best way to assure your safety and foster your power career is to use your brains. When trying a new style, work up slowly, but work hard. I want you to have a good time, but do not ruin it by allowing people or pressure to force you to try something you do not think you can do.

A change in style is often a very positive move. The new movement could breathe new life into your workout and give you more incentive to train, but remember: your safety is the most important thing. You may alter your position over 50 times before you perfect your style. During these adjustments, be aware of danger signs.

Don't just throw the weight on your back and decide to try something new. Give your stance change a lot of thought. Think about what the lift will look like and what you hope to accomplish with it. Take the time to secure your safety, and above all, make changes only when necessary. There is no use messing with a style that is giving you gains. Change your stance when you think it will work for you, but don't make a habit of switching styles before you see if they can help you or not.

Keep your eye on other lifters and learn from their style. If your training goes stale, you may want to try something that somebody else is doing. You can also learn from your current stance. Watch your style and monitor its strengths and weaknesses. It could be that all you need to do is spread your feet or turn your feet a different way. If you are doing well, major revisions should be avoided. There is no sense in redoing something that is bringing you closer to your dream.

My current stance is based on a product of years of experience in practice. I doubt if I will ever change them again, but if the need arises, I will certainly try to. There is no reason to work with a style you are not happy with. You must be satisfied that your style is right for you and that you can expect to make good gains with it.

I witnessed some strange stances during my career. One of the prison lifters shakes his head rapidly from side to side before he starts the deadlift. I swear his head turns completely around the speed he shakes it. Another deadlifter I know lifts with all his back and yet pulls four times his body weight.

It just goes to show that some styles are right for some people. The big thing is to find your style and work with it. My styles have worked for me, and they could be the beginning of your long and happy lifting career as well.

FRANTZ'S SEVENTH COMMANDMENT

"There is no excuse for a lack of practice."

The only way to be successful is to work at it. Success does not come overnight. In order to be the best, you have to give something in return. To be a good powerlifter, you must give your time.

I practice constantly. I do not run myself into the ground, but I do keep my body in peak condition. Many lifters figure if they work heavy twice a month that is good enough to maintain or improve their lifts. I believe, however, that you must keep the pressure on at least two or three times a week or the body will forget what it felt like to do your max.

I am from the old school that believes if you do not hit or try to max at least once a week that you will surely lose it. Strength does not leave your system, but it will take time to get your body adjusted to your max again. The more time you spend getting your system used to your year-old max, the less time can be spent making new gains.

You must set aside at least 3 days per week for powerlifting. It is a good idea to lift at the same time on every lifting day. This way, your system can adjust itself and peak at these times. Your body will actually be looking forward to the time in which you are to be in the gym. Your biological clock will go off, and you will be ready to lift those weights.

There is no excuse for the lack of practice. The only one you can blame for a missed workout is yourself. Before you walk into the gym, you should clear your mind of all thoughts that do not relate to powerlifting. You should focus all of your attention on lifting weights. The second you enter the gym door be thinking nothing but power.

The time in the gym should be spent on improving your lift. You cannot solve family problems or arguments standing under 500 pounds. Practice should be spent practicing. If you're having trouble concentrating, I suggest you do not start your workout until you get your thoughts together.

If you choose not to talk while in the gym, grunt. The main thing is that you work. If you arrived at the gym with a clear mind, stay that way. Do not let problems in the gym affect you. I try never to get involved with gym politics and negative attitudes while I'm working out.

Champions all have one thing in common—they practice. If you want to get better, you're going to have to practice. There is no easy path to success. You'll have to contribute a lot of dreams and some sweat. You cannot expect to be the next champion if you do not act like one.

Another important thing to remember is, during a contest, you have to do all three lifts, so practice them occasionally on the same day. You have to build up your endurance to a level that can sustain the pressure of the big three all in the same time period. Sometimes I will even do them in circuits. I add a little variety to my workout. I suggest that you be very careful when trying this type of workout. Never try to go all-out on all three when you are lifting in this kind of rotation.

In a contest, a good squat and bench will be offset if you are too tired to dead-lift. Practice doing all three, say, once every fourth workout or so. This way, at the meet, it will feel natural to do them together. You won't feel tired, but you will be ready to collect that trophy.

Practice is an important ingredient of power. The amount of work you put into your career will determine the amount of success you will have. I devote enough of my day to make sure I have fully worked my body. It's better to work out a little too much than to slack your training and not develop to your potential. At least when you overwork, you can see it—if you don't work, you can't see anything and that is the sad part.

If you know you will be away from the gym for a couple of extra days, don't be afraid to work out your max . . . and more. You might as well tear your muscles really good and allow the extra time to give them a chance to heal. If I think I'm in a mess, my next workout, I have to the rack and work heavy.

The amount of workouts is important, but the intensity of each workout can mean a lot more. If you exercise daily but don't put much effort into your work, you will never experience elite status. You have to want to work before you can expect to get maximum benefit from your training. I go into the gym with the intention of having a good day, every day.

Learn the value of your workout and you will experience gains beyond belief. Once you have decided what your goals are, do not let anything stand in your way. Practice as often as your body and brain can stand it, because everyone knows, "practice makes perfect."

FRANTZ'S EIGHTH COMMANDMENT

"A good deadlifter will always finish strong."

A good deadlift will win many contests. A lifter can have a poor bench and an average squat and still win with a big deadlift. Some are born with a lot of back strength, but if you were not, do not despair. Practice can give you the big deadlift.

The deadlift has always been one of my strong points. Early in my career, I learned that to be a consistent winner I had to finish strong. I've been in many a contest where I have been a little ahead or behind in the subtotal. In all cases, the deadlift has allowed me to take the trophy home.

A heavy deadlift can psychologically destroy most of the competition. If you open your lift with your opponents' max, it will not only put you on the road to victory, but it will bring down your opposition. The minute a person doubts his ability or his deadlift is the minute you pull ahead.

The Frantz Rocker has given me many proud moments. My problem these days is not getting the weight off the floor, it is keeping my grip once it gets moving. My hands are small and thus, once my grip starts to slip, I have to let go of the bar.

I use straps to hold the bar firmly in my hands. They enable me to lift well over what I could handle with my bare hands. The only problem is they cannot be used in competition so I try not to use them too often. I do not want to get psychologically addicted to using straps when my bare hands have brought me this far.

Unlike most champions, I deadlift heavy at least two times per week. Some lifters say they cannot deadlift heavy two times in a week because it hurts their back. I do not see how, properly done, deadlift can cause that much pain to the back muscles.

With the Frantz Rocker, much of the strength comes from the powerful leg muscles. As the bar passes the knees, you must throw your hips forward. As long as your shoulders are pulled back and you keep driving, your back will not sustain that much pressure.

My theory is that the deadlift, like any other lift, has to be practiced to be mastered. If you do not practice with heavy weights at least (I repeat, *at least*) once per week, you will never get used to handling heavy amounts of iron.

Confidence plays an important role in the deadlift. If you feel you can pull it, you will. The best way to gain confidence is to the experience plenty of heavy dead-lifts in practice. That is what I have been doing ever since my grip failed me in the 1983 Nationals. I have been working the deadlift as my "priority lift" and working the other two lifts after I have satisfied myself that my deadlift routine is finished.

I have even been seeking a solution to my grip problem. I have received plenty of advice from many people, both qualified and unqualified. Some of the sugges-tions included wearing rubber gloves to sweat the fat off my hands and having an operation in getting new hands! I did experiment with a new technique, and I have met with some success.

Before the 1984 Senior State, my wife Diane took a hand grinder and shaved off a good many calluses from my palms. She ground the skin down, and I soaked my hands in ice to keep the swelling down. Then she ground again. I figured she carved at least an eighth of an inch off my hands. My grip did feel a lot more secure during the deadlift after that. I used the strategy during the 1984 Senior Nationals.

I am looking for an 800-pound deadlift in the very near future. It will take a lot of hard work and a great many training sessions, but I plan on reaching my goal. That is what the deadlift takes—work and time. If you are not willing to invest the energy, I suggest you become a bodybuilder.

FRANTZ'S NINTH COMMANDMENT

"Bodybuilding and powerlifting do not mix. Make your choice . . . Beautiful mus-cles or raw power."

It would be great if you had the best-looking set of muscles in the strongest body, both at the same time. Just imagine it—the best of both worlds. You can fly in and win the Olympia, and then run over and capture the World's. That definitely would be something.

Sorry to say that something is a fantasy. There is virtually no way you can be a top bodybuilder and a champion powerlifter at the exact same time. They are two entirely different aspects in the world of iron. You can dream of being Mr. Muscles, but in reality, the likelihood is very slim.

Top bodybuilders usually start out powerlifting to gain the bulk they will later need to look massive. Once a bodybuilder has the bulk, he will usually switch to high-repetition light exercises. This will bring out muscle separation and definition.

A powerlifter who tried to look cut (purely defined) would have to do a good deal of light exercises and go on a strict diet. This would cause his strength to diminish. The purpose of lifting heavy weights is to get strong. The bigger muscle size is a necessary result of the intense straining and exertion done in training. If your goal is power, it would be silly to waste your time cutting up your arms. All that energy could be put into building your legs.

I speak from experience. Early in my career, I called myself an all-round weight lifter. I body built and powerlifted all at the same time. I had some major successes. I was runner-up at the Mr. USA contest . . . not once, but twice.

The only problem was while I was an actively competing powerlifter and a showcase bodybuilder, I could not devote all of my energy into just one. Consequently, I never developed myself to my full potential until I decided I had to choose between beautiful muscles and raw power.

I chose raw power. There's something about going out there and exerting everything I have into one lift that makes one alive. I could feel the power surging through my body. I am the master of my own fate. In bodybuilding, your shape is only as good as the next guy's eyesight. Bodybuilding is a good sport, but power is the only game in town.

Due to my bodybuilding background, I have a good all-around physique. Most pure powerlifters have underdeveloped calves and overdeveloped shoulders. I think that the sacrifice of a few body parts in order to gain power is well worth it. So the powerlifter may have bigger proportioned thighs than he has calves. During the off-season, he can work on his measurements; during the power cycle, he should concentrate on power.

It is impossible to win weight lifting titles unless you train heavy. The only light training you should do is form work, so you can get even heavier. You should not waste your time pumping when you could be building.

You would think with all of the success I have had in powerlifting that I would follow my own advice. But, late in 1983, I did not. After years of experience at being a bodybuilding powerlifter, I made the mistake of trying it again.

I had just come off a best lifter performance in a meet in Wisconsin when I decided to enter the Mr. Illinois contest. I only had 1 week to cut up, but like I said, I have had a lot of bodybuilding experience.

I went on a strict diet. I did not eat for a week. I lay under sunlamps and took my vitamins and did a great deal of stomach work. After 7 days, I was cut to the bone. I felt I looked better than I ever did in the old days.

After a grueling pose down under hot lights, the scores came in. I had finished a disappointing third. I was mad. I was mad at myself for not winning and I was mad at the judges for not seeing the way I felt I should have been seen.

I went back to powerlifting with newfound respect for the sport that treated me well. The 20 pounds I had dropped in order to look cut took its toll. I could not work out for days. I was too weak. It took over 2 months to get my strength back to where it was before the Mr. Illinois contest.

If you want to see your lifts go up, you have to do away with worthless pumping. Concentrate on exercises that will help your bench, squat, and deadlift and most of all, work heavy. Beautiful muscles are fine, but power is what I live for.

FRANTZ'S TENTH COMMANDMENT

"Work with a positive attitude. A winner thinks he can, and a loser never thinks."

When you work with a positive attitude, you can accomplish anything you desire. Being positive is one of the most important steps toward being a champion powerlifter. A positive person is respected both in and out of the gym.

As I approach the bar, I do not tell myself negative thoughts. I do not dwell on the weight or the environment. I think about all the positive workouts that have led me to the contest platform. It would be self-defeating to admit I have doubts.

Doubts are something I do away with in practice. If I doubt I can do a weight, I try to do 10 or 15 pounds more. The second you let doubt alter your strength is the time when you will get three red lights. Uncertainty is the reason why so many lifters missed their attempts.

I try to keep a positive attitude throughout any meet. It is not good for your performance or your mental health to allow negative vibrations to roll your thoughts. If someone lifts a bigger weight than I do, I simply use my second place to spur me into higher goals. If I had won every contest I ever entered, I would have no room for improvement. There would be no reason to strive for higher goals and higher totals.

Competition brings out the best in me. I will be in a big meet, and my blood will be flowing and my muscles aching for a chance to go out there and prove myself. Then when I get my chance, I will run out there and give it all I have got.

I have been in meets, big and small, where the lifters will be warming up in a negative environment. I will see a guy squatting, and he will be complaining about how heavy the weight is. How can a man go through a cycle and psych himself out when it comes time to compete? Backstage, I will get under weight and pump out some easy wraps while telling myself, "Today's the day! Today's the day I show the world what I know I can do."

When warming up at a meet, never choose a heavy weight. If I plan to open 700 in my squat, I will get a few warm-ups in, but I will never go past 650. You have to trust your body and your skills. Do not give your body a chance to feel negative.

If you are negative, you will also attract negatives. The man who moans and groans either lifts with another moaner or works alone. No one likes to hang out with a guy who thinks he can't. Even if you have to lie to yourself in order to make a big lift, do it. It's better to fool yourself for a minute and make the lift instead of admitting your limitations and failing.

When attempting a new high, you have to think you can make it. If you don't think you can, then you won't. Can you imagine walking up to a new max and saying, "Well, I will try it now and make it some other day"? Why try it at all if you're not going to give it your all?

I want you to practice walking up to any weight with "positive confidence." That is why I make my light weights just as if they were my max—you have to practice being positive. You just cannot fly through a system and come to your last set unprepared. Be positive throughout your workout and you will be rewarded with a big total.

Another important distinction is between the positive lifter and the man who lifts and fears. Weight lifting has helped my personality, but it is not my whole life. I have a family and a business to devote time to. I lift because I want to, not because I have to. A lot of guys feel threatened into lifting weights. They fear physical assaults, so they tried to get big. This type of lifter will never become a champion. A person who lifts and fears will always be afraid.

I lift iron because it satisfies a need in me. Lifting keeps me physically fit. It also lets me see the advances I am making in my sport. Unlike basketball where you are only as good as your jump shot, weight lifting allows you to monitor and control your gains. In powerlifting, you control your future and you have no one to blame for your failures.

You have to lift weights because you want to. It is as simple as that. In order to be a champion, you have to want it with all your heart. You also have to plan for it. Again, I stress the need for brain activity during your workout. You cannot expect to reach the top unless you can see it. Know where you are headed in your climb to the top.

A loser never thinks. If you observe a loser, you will notice he never knows what he is going to do next. He just knows that he is going to come short of his expectations. A winner knows what he wants and goes after it. You have to have a plan before you can use the strategy.

In powerlifting, we have the athlete who never seems to know what his next jump is. Ask him what he wants and he says, "What do you think?" This type of person has no idea where life is taking him. All he knows is he won't know what to do once he gets there.

I have trained champions for the better part of 2 decades. As their coach, they will often ask me what they should try next. Because I have trained them and they trust my experience and judgment, I will suggest a weight and they lifted. My lifters are not indecisive; they just trust my judgment.

There comes a time in their careers when they will say, "Ernie, I want to try this weight and you watch—I will make it." When I start to hear this, then I know the lifter has mastered my Ten Commandments.

The most important thing I can give a lifter is a positive program. A system that will give him a chance to make new highs that I can offer. The most important thing a person can bring to powerlifting is a positive attitude. The two, together, will eventually produce a champion.

Jose Garcia, Ahmad 'Joe' Atef, Ernie Frantz, Ray Makiejus

Matthew Penrose, Ahmad 'Joe' Atef, Ernie Frantz, Howard Penrose, Ray Makiejus

Ernie Frantz and Joe Weider

ALL-OR-NONE CONCEPT

Often I see lifters pumping out their reps. They look like pistons pumping up and down, faster and faster, until they cannot get another rep. The system is just great. The pump you will develop will make you feel like Mr. Universe. Your muscles will even increase in size.

The only problem is, once the blood goes away, so will your muscles. Pumping all the blood through your body will give you a terrific psychological high, but it won't give you strength. If your goal is power, pumping muscles will do you little, if any, good.

Powerlifting does not pump your muscles; powerlifting tears them down. Lifting a heavy weight will put a strain on your muscles so that the fibers will actually rip. When these torn muscles recuperate, they will be bigger and stronger than ever.

Your muscles will be ready to take more strain as long as you let them rest from the previous workout. After several months, or years, of this, your body will be stronger and bigger than you had ever dreamed it could be. Powerlifting builds a strong physical foundation. It is the only sport where a man can look like a mountain.

The trick is to use heavy weights to break the fibers, and then plenty of rest in order to amend them. I rarely work the same lift heavy 2 days in a row. The muscles just are not healed enough to accept all that strain again. If you lift on torn muscles, they will never heal properly. What will happen is you'll actually get weaker instead of growing stronger. How can you grow if all your muscles are broken up from lifting heavy iron? You have to let yourself rest.

In powerlifting, you rarely feel the pump that a bodybuilder experiences. In powerlifting, our high comes from lifting heavier and heavier weights. When I reach a new goal and set a new max, I am so happy I feel as though I have won the lottery. The bodybuilder gets his high from blood rushing through his body. We get our contentment from knowing we are stronger today than we were yesterday.

Bodybuilders spend several hours a day pumping out set after set and rep after rep. They do not stop until they drop. A powerlifter should have a good hour and a half to devote to his workout. The powerlifter should conserve his strength for the big lift. The bodybuilder can afford to pump out those extra reps with a light weight; the powerlifter has to respect his poundage.

I currently use a 4-day schedule. I lift on Monday, Tuesday, Thursday, and Saturday. I go heavy every day except for Tuesday. I use this day as a pickup for a lift that may be lagging or as a form day. I will usually do two lifts at a time.

If I squat, I will also deadlift. I do this because the squat warms me up so I can jump right into heavy deadlifts. If I deadlift before I squat, I will have to spend extra sets making sure my body is prepared for the poundage assault I'm going to put on it.

I try to get all three lifts in on Monday and Thursday. If I get all three in on Monday, I will use Tuesday for late squats and deadlifts. When I squat and deadlift on Monday, I will bench on Tuesday. I do not get all three on Thursday. I'll make time to come back and bench at another time of the day.

Saturday is my extremely heavy day. I always do all three lifts to the extreme then. I will spend the whole day at my gym working the big three. I will try new maxes and do as many negatives and heavy singles as I think my body can stand. I do not let anything interfere with my Saturdays. There are times I will try to lift until I drop. On Saturday, I always try to push myself to the limit.

Now for the big question: How many reps and heavy sets should you do? Weight lifters of all types have been debating this question as far back as time goes. Below is my opinion after years of experimentation. You should warm up until you feel ready to make your jumps. Then I suggest you make big jumps until you are within 100 pounds of your max. From there, a jump of 40 or 50 pounds and another 30 pounds should properly prepare your body to handle your max. The idea is to reach your high weights swiftly, but safely. You do not want to waste your strength doing a lot of weights know won't test you. You should jump big until you're within that heavy zone, then you can jump small and achieve success.

Once you've hit around your max, you can decide if you want or need more. If your body feels strong, then you may decide to try for a new high. The key is to reach your max with enough energy left over to make the decision. If you do too many mediocre sets, you will be too tired to hit a new high.

I judge the number of my sets by instinct. If I feel good, I will go higher and make bigger jumps. One thing I will never do is jeopardize my safety. I always make sure I am ready to head toward my max. It makes no sense to try to go heavy until you're satisfied that your light lifts have given you that positive feeling to continue.

Now for the other tough decisions that all lifters face. I feel one rep is all you need per set. That is, all your body needs—except on the first few sets of warm-ups. One sounds like a quick and easy number and it should be.

When I start a lift, and I will warm up with a light weight for six or eight reps. This will put a little blood in the area and warm it up for future shocks. My next set may consist of two or three reps, but after that a single is all I do.

Some champions feel that you have to do doubles or triples to promote muscle growth. I disagree! I believe in the all-or-none concept. I have tried every system known to man, and yet, I have always returned to the "heavy single."

If you are lifting a heavy amount of weight and it does not tear your muscle fibers on the first rep, I suggest you rack it and put on more iron. A good heavy single will tear all the fibers that need to be torn. After that, you are placing yourself at an unnecessary injury risk. There is no reason why someone should try for another rep with a heavy weight. If the weight was heavy enough to tax your muscles, you should not be able to do another rep with good form. If the weight is not heavy enough to tax your muscles, then there is no sense in doing more reps.

There is also psychological gain from the one-rep system. At a contest, people are not interested in how many reps you can do. All the judges want to see is your heaviest lift for one rep.

I have seen lifters do five reps with 600 in the gym, and then at the meet time, only do a 620-pound single. You have to lift in practice as though it was the real thing. Habits, even bad, that you pick up in practice, are what you're going to display in a meet.

If you like to rep, your body and mind will not be ready for heavy singles. When you are cycling for a contest, you have to limit yourself to a one rep per set.

PSYCHOLOGICAL BLOCKS

Powerlifting is a mind game. You must believe in yourself before you can make gains. A person must not be able to see future gains before they happen. If you cannot see yourself as a champion, how do you expect to ever get there? You must have, and keep, a vision of success.

Many lifters have psychological blocks when it comes to one of the big three. Most develop blocks toward a deadlift. They cannot picture their back lifting that much iron. One's inability to draw mental pictures will eventually be his powerlifting weak point.

You can have the strongest body in the world, but if your mind is weak, you will be too. You have to be able to picture yourself successfully heaving a new max. If you're blind to your own dreams, they will never be reality. The only way to handle psychological barriers is to tackle them head-on. If you have a fear toward the deadlift, I suggest you bombard yourself with heavy singles and heavier negatives. You want to be able to make the deadlift your pet exercise. You should practice at first—this way, you will be fresh and have all your mental juices to work with.

Once fatigue sets in, you can trick yourself out of the lift simply by blaming it on your exhausted condition. If the lift is lagging, put it at the top of your schedule and work hard. If you feel a psychological block coming on, work through it. I should say—fight it. Use every ounce of strength you have to get over it.

If the squat is giving you problems and your max is not coming with any consistency, I suggest you try something different. You can widen your stance, change your hand position, or alter your downward speed, but do something. Just do not sit there and let your max slip away before your eyes.

Negatives are a great way of getting over mental snags. Say you are stuck at 300 on the bench, just as a pattern breaker, try negative with 325. When you see how easy 325 is, you will blow past 300. This overload system works because your body relies on the impressions of your mind.

Hang up pictures of the lift you're having trouble with and look at them daily. Picture yourself doing the lift. Keep forcing mental images of the successful lift through your thoughts. If you're stuck in traffic or early for an appointment, take the time to mentally rehearse the lift.

After all the concentration you have given to the weaker lift, you will be dying to get to the gym. You will not be able to wait until you get the bar in your hands. You will be hungry for success. Nothing will deter you from having a good day.

Forced reps is also a good way to fight through block. Drop down a set, then ask a partner to put his hand on the bar. Now pump out a few reps and ask him to help when and if needed. Just by the presence of his hand on the bar, your mind will think the weight is lighter; consequently, your body will do a good set.

The only problems with forced reps are you have to have a good spotter and you do not want to get psychologically dependent on help. Good spotters are a must and in any set, particularly when you're doing forced reps. You make your body grind out reps; if your body rejects or stalls during the movement, injury may occur. The idea is to break a block, not to hurt yourself. I suggest you pick spotters you feel comfortable with.

Another problem is becoming dependent on the help of another. It's easy to tell yourself you did not do that much work on a particular rep. Forced reps are supposed to prove to your mind what your body can do. Do not let them further complicate your cause by making you dependent on help before you can finish a lift. Make your body fight is an excellent method for defeating a psychological block, but be on guard for signs of dependency.

You can plant psychological blocks in other lifters by being negative or by being overly positive. Your particular attitude at a meet can affect the environment to such an extent that you can force bad performances.

If you're in a contest or at an important practice, you can actually depress and deflate most of your opposition simply by telling them how sluggish they look. I often see lifters running around a contest telling everybody else that they look skinny or tired.

These comments never bother me because I train hard and I know my abilities. I do see where they have their effect on the less-experienced lifter. I can also get to the lifter who knows he is not in his best possible physical condition.

This trick of using words on your competition is an old one. Sorry to say, it is alive and could be heard in most weight lifting competitions. The best way to avoid falling into this trap is to be in the best shape possible. That means mentally and physically ready to win.

Another way to create blocks is to be overly positive. Walk around the meet with a smile on your face, stop and examine the first-place trophy, and pass out a lot of compliments. When you warm up, make a lot of noise. Talk about how light the weight feels. The other lifters will be stunned and amazed with your positive confidence. It may rattle them enough to throw them off the rhythm and give you a victory.

Remember, in a contest when you post your openers, you're allowed to change them before the weight gets to your poundage and before your name is called. It would not hurt to post your correct bench, but then to inflate the deadlift by 50 or 100 pounds or so.

Your opposition will go through the whole meet thinking they're going to lose in the deadlift. This may hamper the squat and bench. They may either get depressed and bomb or try to catch your imaginary deadlift and miss their second or third lift.

When it comes time to deadlift reduce your opener. Make sure you do at least 20 pounds before it comes up. Either that or watch the cards—at any rate, do not get called over the loudspeaker or you will have to open higher. This game of misrepresenting your openers is a good one, but do not overuse or abuse it.

Mental blocks can put an end to a good powerlifting career. Make sure you recognize and fight them before they defeat you. There is one more way to fight a mental block, but I'm hesitant to include it here. If you feel a block coming on, you can rest from that lift or lifting altogether, but beware that you do not accidentally end your powerlifting career in doing so.

The rest will give you total recuperation and hopefully give you a burning desire to return to the gym more to that particular lift. For instance, if you're lifting on the bench, then skip the bench day. The missed workout should make you anxious to get on the bench during the next workout. Hopefully, you can channel this anxiety into a new high.

The only thing is that you must first master my seventh commandment. There is no excuse for the lack of practice. If you choose to use rest as an extreme motivator for a missing workout, you better tell yourself you will work twice as hard on your next gym visit. If you avoid the lift or lifting altogether for too many days, you may find yourself as an ex-lifter.

If you plan to gain entrance into the powerlifters Hall of Fame, you will need to work hard. There is no other way to achieve success but through constant applications of proven techniques. There will be times in your lifting career when you think another game will never come. You have to fight through these stagnant periods. If you let slow times get you down you will never catch your peak. Sometimes the need to improve your lifts will drain you of all your mental and physical juices, but do not despair. Just follow the thoughts I have outlined in this book and "keep on pushing." Every day a powerlifter gets stronger and stronger. It just seems that some of those days are longer than others.

CYCLES AND GOALS

The worst thing a powerlifter can do is fall into a rut. When powerlifters hit plateaus in their lifts, it seems as if they never had experienced gains. Lifters will get depressed and act as though the world is over. This feeling of going nowhere has ended many powerlifting careers, and if you don't understand it, it might negatively affect yours.

Most lifters will never recover from a major rut. The true champion will work through them. You have to keep driving, even though your lifts are not headed anywhere. You cannot quit striving to better yourself just because you are not seeing daily gains.

The best way to fight the rut is through the use of cycles and goals. I have mastered both of these concepts. In over 2 decades of powerlifting I had to. Without the cycle and the use of goals, your training would have no meaning and, thus, be vulnerable to sticking points. Sooner or later, you will quit lifting altogether.

If I had made a 5-pound gain a week throughout my career, my total would now be 7,200 pounds. That would be outstanding. Compared to that inflated number, my actual 2,000 (at a body weight of 198 pounds in 1984) seems small. The truth is, you just cannot expect to make monthly, weekly, or daily gains. The body has its limits. If a powerlifter squatted every day and did nothing else, you would expect his squat to go up. How high can his squat go? That depends on his cycles and his goals. Their max would depend on their "plan of action."

If a lifter has no goals, they also have no way of measuring their progress. I have always had goals. That is why I am still a competitive powerlifter even after all these years. My long powerlifting career is not a string of luck victories, but a collection of planned successes.

One of my goals was to win the Nationals again, and then take on the World once more. I came within 5 pounds of doing that in 1983 when my grip in the deadlift failed me. I realized I was 50 years old, but I was 49 when I finished a close second. Age does not matter as much as the desire to reach your goals. I could be 100 years old, and if I wanted to, I could still set powerlifting goals and—work toward them. So can you.

Goals enable the powerlifter to plot his progress. You can sit down and decide how strong you will be by the beginning of the year and at the end of the next. Then you can take these goals and work toward them. Goals allow a person to establish future trends. Without goals, lifting would be less structured and, thus, more vulnerable to sticking points.

I use short- and long-term goals. One of my short-term goals is to improve my grip in the deadlift. A long-term goal was to squat 900 pounds at 220 pounds of body weight. Both of these goals were realistic because I thought about them before I set them.

By using short-term goals, I keep myself alert and climbing toward higher totals. The use of long-term goals helps turn dreams into reality. By putting the future down on paper, I can better plot a plan of action. I try never to "lift blind" but to have a certain direction in mind. To be successful at anything, you have to figure out a way to obtain your desires or each of your goals.

Goals enable you to visually see your successes. If you want to improve your squat by 100 pounds, you have to see it, and then set the goal to meet it. Now, when you have a plan, you can better work toward it. If you were to enter the gym and every workout try to squat that 100-pound gain on your squat, eventually you will either injure yourself or get sick of missing the same weight during every workout.

It is not advisable to constantly strive for higher and higher totals. Sure, the first couple of months the gains will come easy. Then, after the first year, your total will be respectable, but if you do not give your mind and your body a rest, you might regress. It makes no sense to keep pouring it on when your body cannot take it. Rest is just as important as heavy weights when it comes to being prepared for a contest.

The mind and body need a break from the constant tension caused by trying to excel every time you are in the gym. I am not saying slack off and miss lifts intentionally. I am telling you to use the cycle. Your body is not a mechanical machine. You need more than an occasional oil change before you can expect to operate at peak efficiency.

The cycle allows you to work toward your goals. I usually use a 9-week cycle when training for all major meets. The first week, I establish my maxes. I then slowly turn it on. Every workout I try heavier and heavier weights. I overload the body with tremendous pressure. I also eat well and get a lot of sleep. At the end of my cycle, I will post my totals at the meet, and then take a well-deserved rest. I will usually take 2 or 3 days off after the meet. I consider this a reward for a cycle well done.

When I get back to training I will still lift heavy but not with the same intensity. The cycle throws me in a higher gear, but I cannot stay in it for very long. Eventually, I will be physically and mentally exhausted. I will not have any reserves. I will actually run out of gas. When the cycle is over, I will have to give my body a chance to fully recuperate. That means that I will have to cut back on my level of intensity.

Some lifters cycle only one or two times a year. I am so used to my powerlifting trends that I can cycle three or four times a year and still make good gains. Remember, you have to listen to your body. In over 20 years of powerlifting, the longest layoff I have ever "willingly" taken is 5 days.

I enjoy training heavy and miss not working out. My expectations will not let me. A long-term goal of mine is to live the rest of my life cycling. The only way for me to end my lift on a cycle is to be successful on my present cycles. Only time will tell if I reach this dream.

Before you set any goals, you have to use your brain. Don't set a goal because you want to make it; set a goal because you *can* make it. For instance, I want to squat 1,000 pounds, but I set my goal at 900 pounds. A thousand would be a dream, but 900 is closer to reality. I realize some people find it easier to look toward big chores, but trying to reach an impossible dream will only give you an excuse for failing. Try to set your goals with success in mind.

The length of your cycle should be determined by your abilities and your stamina. You shouldn't really worry about cycling until you have hit a rut in your lifts. Novices should turn it on until their bodies signal that they need to rest. Once a person hits the rut, they should evaluate their lifting. If you have good endurance and feel strong, you might want to go on a 12-week cycle. If you feel weak but have a contest coming up, you can choose a shorter cycle. The important thing is to know your limitations and to work to expand them.

The cycle can be the lifter's friend . . . or his worst enemy. What the cycle does for you depends on how you treat it. When I start my cycle, I really start. I don't timidly lift a little more weight. I aggressively attack those weights with gains in my eyes. I know what I expect from the cycle, and I work hard toward my goals. You can't expect to make gains unless you really want to with all your heart and energy.

You should have at least one goal for every cycle you go on. It is not very smart to start your acceleration period without any short-term plans. Before I start a cycle, I will sit down and decide what I hope to gain from this venture. When I started my cycle for the 1984 Senior Nationals, I already knew what I planned to lift at the end of that cycle, and I had not even started it yet. For the Nationals, I planned to squat 850 pounds, bench 450 pounds, and deadlift 800 pounds.

These are realistic goals because I had thought them over since my second-place finish back in 1983. I planned to start my cycle soon and worked hard toward those marks. The important thing is that I had goals. Those goals gave me the direction I needed to again find that winner's platform. A 1,200 pound total at 198 pounds would also add another chapter to my long career.

You will eventually get very good at setting your goals and starting your cycles, but for now, practice these methods. Try to learn more about you as a person and as a lifter. Eventually, you will be able to easily decide your goals and the proper time to reach them, but for now, be happy that you are using some thought during your lifting. These methods can give you an edge over your competition because you are not only using your muscles, but your head, as well.

THE FRANTZ ROUTINE

To summarize what I have already written, I try to do all three lifts on Monday, Thursday, and Saturday. I use Tuesday for light squats and deadlifts or as a bench day if I do not bench on Monday. I rest on Wednesday, Friday, and Sunday. Sometimes I will use the power rack on Tuesdays, but usually I do not. I try to go extra heavy on Saturday.

MONDAY
SQUAT

145 x 8	This is really light, but a good warm-up.
235 x 6	Again, I'm just warming up.
325 x 3	I'm trying to make easy jumps.
415 x 1	I have to do extra sets, but it's worth it.
505 x 1	The weight is still light.
595 x 1	I will wrap for this set.
685 x 1	Now, I know I'm working.
740 x 1	I will wrap and suit up.
780 x 1	This will set me up for 800-plus.
810 x 1	This is the money set.
820 x 1D	My down set to test the weight.

DEADLIFT

245 x 3	Already warmed up from squats.
335 x 1	Can jump a little faster.
475 x 1	Easy, but psyching me for the big day.
575 x 1	Trying to concentrate on 800.
675 x 1	This set will determine how high I go.
725 x 1	I want to make this every try.
775 x 1	I usually use straps for this one.
800 x 1	May use straps or negative it.

BENCH

145 x 8	Trying to warm up.
235 x 6	I try to watch my shoulders.
325 x 2	I am ready to jump.
375 x 2	Every rep is a strict one.
415 x 1	I know I am working now.
440 x 1	Usually my high for the day.
460 x 3N	If I have enough energy.

TUESDAY
SQUAT

145 x 8	Warmed up a bit from yesterday.
255 x 5	Looking to work, but not to hurt.
365 x 2	Trying to work with form.
480 x 1	This set will determine how high I go.
580 x 1	I will wrap for this set.
660 x 1	Time for the full treatment.
720 x 1	I try to use good form.
750 x 1	Heavy, but easy compared to Monday.
625 x 7B	I try to do seven perfect bottoms.

DEADLIFT

245 x 3	A set to get used to form.
335 x 1	I try to pull this one fast.

475 x 1   The Frantz Rocker works!

600 x 1   Feeling tired but optimistic.

660 x 1   Pull this one and take a day off.

WEDNESDAY

Day of rest and recuperation . . .

THURSDAY
SQUAT

145 x 8   Light but effective.

255 x 5   Still testing muscles.

385 x 1   Now, I'm ready to jump.

475 x 1   This one should be easy.

565 x 1   I wrap from here on.

655 x 1   I put my suit up.

730 x 1   Try to go deep.

780 x 1   Setting myself up for the 800s.

815 x 1   Good enough for today.

DEADLIFT

245 x 3   Warm up for safety.

355 x 1   Still getting used to form.

485 x 1   Now, I'm ready to jump.

600 x 1   This will determine how strong I feel.

680 x 1   Should be easy.

740 x 1   Have to work for my money.

790 x 1   The end of a good day.

BENCH

145 x 8   Warming up again.

235 x 5   I'm ready to go now.

325 x 2   Making sure the shoulders work.

380 x 1   I get a big arch and push.

400 x 1   Trying to get heavy singles.

420 x 1	I use perfect form.
440 x 1	This is my good set.
450 x 1	I try to push this one.

FRIDAY

I try to totally relax on Friday. I spend the whole day looking forward to my heavy Saturday. I usually eat a lot on Fridays and try to bulk up on the calories so I can put them to good use on the following day.

SATURDAY
SQUAT

145 x 8	Warming up to bigger things.
255 x 5	Getting ready for the jumps.
400 x 1	Trying to really get into it.
500 x 1	At this point I know if it's a good day.
600 x 1	I wrap this set on.
700 x 1	I use the suit.
750 x 1	I try to go deep in the pocket.
800 x 1	This now comes every Saturday.
820 x 1	I work for this one.
840 x 1	I give it all I have.
870 x 1D	I feel this for the future.

DEADLIFT

245 x 3	I'm warming up.
360 x 1	I'm ready and willing.
480 x 1	Here go the jumps.
580 x 1	At this point I'm ready for more.
660 x 1	This pulls easy.
720 x 1	This one requires some work.
760 x 1	A nice steady move.
780 x 1	I may use straps.
810 x 1	I really want to feel this one.

BENCH

145 x 6	Warming up for a big day.
255 x 3	Trying to get there fast.
345 x 1	I'm ready to try some heavy ones.
390 x 1	Strict and quick.
415 x 1	I'm on a psychological high.
435 x 1	I try to muscle it up.
445 x 1	Want this one bad.
460 x 1	Give it my all.
480 x 3N	Fight like hell.
350 x 10S	I'm winded but ready for one more.
300 x 20S	At last the day is over.

This is the extent of the Frantz lifting week. As you can tell, I "work hard," but I have to. I have a lot invested in my powerlifting career, and I have yet to reach my maximum output. I still want to officially post a 2,000 pound total in the 198-pound weight class. At the time I trained at 210 pounds, but if the gains keep coming at this weight, it was be easy to drop the 12 pounds and reach my total. I have registered a 1,940 pound or better on several occasions.

I do not make the same jumps every week. What weight I choose depends on how I feel and what day it is. I always try to push myself on Saturday, because I psych myself for that day throughout the week. As for Monday and Thursday, I try to hit as close to my max, if not my max, on each day. When I told you I poured it on, I meant it. The secret to becoming a champion is an easy one—work hard. That does not sound like much of a secret, but you would be surprised at the amount of lifters who refuse to acknowledge those two little words. *Work Hard!*

The reason why I do so many sets is because my maximum poundages are so high. A 500 squatter can arrive at his max a lot faster than I can, but that does not upset me. Sometimes, I will get frustrated and jump high and fast. I try not to allow myself to get impatient too often. The extra sets it requires me to reach my high are often light, so I use them for confidence builders. I try not to do a lot of heavy singles if I am trying to establish my max because heavy singles will sap my strength and make the odds on my hitting a new high very slim.

If I want to do heavy singles, I will walk into the gym with this intention. It can be dangerous to try your max after a long series of heavy singles. Don't get me wrong, a lot of lifters like to work out in this manner, but I do stress caution. It's best to go to the gym with one goal in mind. This way, your body will know what direction you are headed. If you want to do a lot of singles, I advise you to hit your max, and then drop down and start your reps.

I usually wrap for the squat from the 600 mark on. I can successfully squat 600 without wraps, but I feel more secure and confident with the elastic feeling that comes with wraps. This secure feeling will later help me to squat my max. During the week, I squat with a fairly tight suit, but on Saturday, I squeeze into the smallest suit I can. I also wear different shoes on Saturday.

I feel the change in equipment allows me to get into a different frame of mind. For some reason, when Saturday comes around, I am ready to do my best. The reason is, I prepare for it. I monitor my progress by this big day. If I have too many weak Saturdays in a row, I know I'm doing something wrong. I can then start to alter my routine and get myself back on the right track. I suggest every lifter devise a "progress checker." Whether it be a certain heavy day or a certain lift, it is a smart move to have some regular routine to check your overall progress by.

I rarely use my suit or my wraps in the deadlift. I find them too restricting for the Frantz Rocker, so I simply deadlift without them. When it comes time for a contest, I will deadlift in a loose-fitting suit. A tight suit will force my shoulders in and make it hard for me to lock out. To test if your suit is too restricting, try to pull your shoulders back before you start to deadlift. If you cannot, than your suit is too tight for the deadlift.

The same thing applies to the bench. If my suit is tight it will restrict my arch and more than likely leave the weight sitting on my chest. When I bench, I try to pay close attention to my shoulders because I have experienced too many shoulder tears in the past. That is why my bench is not on par with my other two lifts. I am now slowly bringing my bench back to respectability. Even with all of my power knowledge, I just can't seem to avoid tearing my shoulders. One of the secrets to my powerlifting longevity is—I keep my progress charted. I write down all my workouts and later compare them to my past workouts. In this way, I can monitor my progress and plan future workouts. It would be nonsense to lift and forget. You can learn from a workout even when it is over. I have a giant black book in which I record all of my attempts. Those who forget past workouts are doomed to repeat them.

Another useful instrument for charting your progress is the Frantz Powergraf. This graph can keep track of your monthly gains. All you have to do is post your best lift for the month and after a couple of months you can see a pattern starting to develop. These lines will tell you how fast your lifts are progressing and which lift is growing the fastest. This way, you will be able to control long-range goals.

SUPPLEMENTS

There are several things for power: You must strain to tear muscle tissue, you must rest to repair them, and you must get the proper amount of nutrition to allow your muscles to recuperate and grow. A powerlifter lacking in nutrition cannot expect to continue making gains.

Just like a plant needs sun, a powerlifter needs protein. Our body is made up for protein. We must constantly replenish this supply daily in order to function effectively. If you were to eliminate protein from your diet, you would find yourself constantly tired and weak. You would have no energy. Needless to say, you would also have no muscles.

It is important to eat complete proteins. These proteins contain all of your essential amino acids. Complete proteins trigger the process that will eventually yield you stronger muscle tissue. A few complete proteins are most meat and cheese products.

Generally, you should get at least half of your body weight in grams of protein. Say you weigh 200 pounds, then you should ingest at least 100 grams of protein. I like to take this amount in protein supplement (powder form), and then go ahead and eat a balanced diet. This way, I can be always sure that my protein intake is high.

Everybody's metabolism is different. It seems like the older I get, the more protein I need to take. I always start the day with a protein drink (I manufacture my own mix). The protein drink will assure me that I am waking up on the right side of the bed.

Many of your champion bodybuilders and powerlifters will confess to taking huge quantities of protein, vitamins, and minerals. I am not one of them. I feel that you can get most of your daily requirements through a balanced diet. The sad thing is that in this technological world it is hard to eat a balanced meal. Fast-food restaurants and high-priced health food are slowly making a balanced diet a rarity in American society.

For this reason, I do keep a supply of vitamins on hand. Some vitamins cannot be produced or stored by our body. Vitamin C is one element that must be taken on a daily basis. Periodically, I will take high doses of vitamins. These sprees tend to lift my spirits and give new life to my system. I do not like to take large qualities of vitamins while I am on a cycle or on a workout day. I feel my system cannot effectively handle the stress of the weight if my body is busy digesting and utilizing supplements.

A word of caution about supplements—you can get too much of a good thing. Just because supplements are healthy does not mean it is healthy to take huge doses. There is no need to overdo a successful formula.

Many lifters go on a high-protein diet. They ingest hundreds of grams of protein daily. Sure, their protein levels will always be sufficient, but their wallets will be always empty. Protein is expensive. If your carbohydrates are low, you will have to use protein as a source of energy.

Your body cannot repair itself if it's starved for fluids. I suggest you drink at least six glasses of water per day. If you start to bloat, cut down on your intake, but make sure you keep replenishing your system. You don't want to leave your system dry while you are trying to build it up.

Too much of one vitamin or mineral can also throw your system off. Each element represents a spot on an imaginary teeter-totter. If one element is excessive or deficient, the whole system will become unstable. It does not make any sense to load up on vitamin B when you are deficient in A, C, D, etc.

I like to go on a food fast at least twice a month. I give my digestive system a couple of days off. After a 1- or 2-day fast, I feel lighter, happier, and more important, stronger. During these voluntary food strikes, I drink a great deal of liquids and continue my life at a normal pace. I try not to fast on lifting days because the shock to the body from the lack of food and heavy weights could be dangerous.

Your digestive system is at work 24 hours a day. Even when your body is resting on the outside, it is working on the inside. Depriving your body of food, for a short period, can give your system a chance to rest and recharge itself. This test period may be all you need to continue your powerlifting gains.

I suggest you use supplements to your own advantage. Find out what you want out of powerlifting and build a nutrition program to fit your needs. I urge you to read the labels, ask questions, and learn how your body works.

The best way to determine if a nutrition program is right for you is to simply watch the scale and your mood changes. By watching your weight, you will see the actual outcome of a certain program. If you start to put on a lot of weight but no strength, this may be an indication that your nutrition choices are not fulfilling your physical strength requirements. You have to watch your mood swings. Vitamin C might make you a happier person, but you will never know until you try.

Not everyone has to take a protein supplement in powder form, but it is a good idea. Powdered protein is a "powerlifter's insurance policy" against deficient protein levels. You cannot grow without gas, so make sure that you have enough protein to allow your body to repair itself and, thus, to grow stronger. The only way to reach your dreams is to plan for them. Plan an intelligent nutrition program and you will be on your way.

THE DIET

You could work out from now until forever and never get big unless you have the proper rest and nutrition. One of the keys to success is having enough energy to accomplish your goals. It makes no sense to go through your routine only to stall on your big lift. You have to have enough energy to reach your goal, and then enough energy left to enjoy your status.

I get most of my strength through the protein foods. Protein foods are most meats, cheeses, eggs, and assorted canned goods that are made to give you the nourishment tired muscles beg for. I try to eat balanced meals, but I have a secret weapon in case I do not.

My insurance that I will meet my energy needs is my protein powder. I manufacture my supplement with all the necessary amino acids and vitamins to give me the lift I need. One heaping tablespoon can supply me with roughly 25 grams of muscle-building protein. My recipe for a concoction that will lift you up is as follows:

5 heaping tablespoons of protein powder

2 eggs

1 banana (for potassium)

1 glass of milk

2 ice cubes

I drink this mixture daily. It can add weight if I drink it after a meal or take weight off if I drink it in a place of meal. Either way, it assures me that my body is getting the fuel it needs to run on. This is very important because you can't be sure you are getting your proper nutrition through food.

Occasionally, I am guilty of sneaking in too much junk food. Sometimes I will rationalize my habit by saying I use junk food as a source for carbohydrates. The truth is, I can find better energy sources to fit my needs, but I love pizza, cake, candy . . .

Junk food (popcorn, candy, chocolates, etc.) can be used as a source for energy, but I advise you not to stuff yourself on otherwise worthless calories. Junk foods contain a great deal of sugar, and sugar is of no value to your body. In fact, you lose precious vitamins because your system is forced to digest all the worthless sugar you ingest. Therefore, large amounts of junk food will hurt your lifting by giving you false energy and draining you of otherwise quality nutrients.

Instead of getting energy from junk food, I try to get it from fruit. Fruit also contains sugar, but not in the white powder form. Fruit contains fructose, a more natural sugar that can be more easily assimilated into your system. Fruit is a lot healthier than junk but—too much fruit can be harmful to your lifting. Much of it can produce acid in your stomach, which will, of course, deter you from reaching your powerlifting goals.

My mother's side of the family is Italian, and all my life I have been treated to big old-fashioned Italian dinners. To this day, I still have no problems gorging myself on Mother's cooking. Sometimes, however, even too much of a good thing can be bad for you. It is not healthy to eat big meals unless you plan to work hard.

I try not to eat a heavy meal before I lift. Too much food in my stomach will give me stuffed and a satisfied feeling. These feelings will take away from the drive I need to lift my best. That goes the same for water. Do not drink large amounts of fluids if you are planning to work out. The excess liquid will give you a bloated feeling and, thus, take away from your weight lifting performance.

There is no set rule on how much weight you can gain or lose at one time. Everybody's metabolism is different. I could eat a five-course meal and gain 10 pounds. You could eat the same meal and your structure would only pack on 2 or 3 pounds. The key is to learn about your body. Find out what different foods do to your system and how they affect your lifting performance.

Some experts say that you can only gain an average of 8 pounds of muscle per year. In other words, if you put on 20 pounds this year, according to them, only 8 of it will be muscle and the other 12 will be fat. I cannot agree with this. I have seen lifters put on 20 pounds and look great. These same lifters experienced a tremendous jump in their overall totals. I feel the following equation will determine how much muscle you can put on in any given year.

work + diet + rest + metabolism = growth

It is never healthy to put on or to take off large amounts of weight too quickly. Drastic increases or decreases in your body weight can shock your system and leave it unresponsive to your training. No matter what your physique goals are, start out slowly and closely monitor your progress.

A lot of lifters train at 5 or 10 pounds above their weight class limitations. I would have been lifting in the 198-pound class and I trained at 203 to 207 pounds of body weight. There is a big reason for this—the increased body weight enables you to handle heavier loads of iron. When it comes time for a contest, I simply drop down to 198 and try my best to win.

Quick losses of body weight will hurt your lifting. Your body cannot do its best if you drain it of all its nutrition. You will not able to lift your heaviest if you starve your system of much-needed protein. The idea is not to lose weight too quickly when you are on your cycle. You have to feed your body as you strive for power.

The way I safely drop my weight to meet my class is to temporarily drain my system of its retained fluids. I have mastered this process through decades of experimentation. I advise you to read my words carefully and exercise caution if you plan on using this method of losing weight.

Toward the end of my cycle, I will build up my electrolytes with potassium. This will assure me that my joints will not lock up when it comes time to shed my water. I will continue to eat until the very day of the contest, but the day before the event I will restrict my fluid intake. In other words, keep eating, but stay off the liquids.

The night before the contest I might take a few diuretics to drop fluid weight if I feel I have to lose over 5 pounds to meet my class restriction. In the morning, I stay away from all foods and drinks until I have weighed in the meet. Once I have made weight, I take a sodium (salt) pill, and then start to slowly put fluids back to my system. Your fluid level varies with the amount of salt in your body. You must replace the salt because you can expect your body to take back those precious fluids. One without the other will mean that you are in trouble.

At first, this whole concept might seem absurd to you. But again, I remind you, I speak from experience. I can safely take off up to 8 pounds of body weight the night before a contest. Those 8 pounds might be the difference between coming in first in the 198- or last in the 220-pound class.

My confidence in this system helps it works for me. I have done it before, and I know that I can do it again. After I slowly put back in the fluids I took out, I find my strength has not changed at all. The only thing is that I can only do this with 8 pounds or less. If I have to lose more than 8 pounds, I feel drained, as if my system is already exhausted before the meet starts.

Remember to eat a balanced meal and monitor your bodily reaction to changes in your diet. If you want to be a champion, you have to eat like one. The only way to know if you are eating properly is to watch how your body feels. It is important to learn how to listen to your body; it might tell you how to be that champion.

PROTEIN GUIDE

		Calories	Protein	Carbohydrates
Milk, Cheese, Cream				
Milk:				
Whole	1 cup	160	9	12
Skim	1 cup	60	9	12
Buttermilk	1 cup	90	9	12
Evaporated (unsweetened)	1 cup	345	18	24
Evaporated (sweetened)	1 cup	980	25	166
Cheese:				
Blue or Roquefort	1 oz.	105	6	1
Cheddar	1 oz.	115	7	1
Cottage	12 oz.	360	46	10
Cream	8 oz.	850	18	5
American	1 oz.	105	7	1
Camembert	1⅓ oz.	115	7	1
Parmesan	1 oz.	130	12	1
Swiss	1 oz.	105	8	1
Pasteurized Process Cheese Spread	1 oz.	80	5	2
Cream:				
Half and Half	1 cup	325	8	11
Light	1 cup	505	7	10
Whipping Cream (light)	1 cup	715	6	9
Whipping Cream (heavy)	1 cup	840	5	7
Powdered Creamer	1 cup	505	4	52

(Continued)

PROTEIN GUIDE (*Continued*)

		Calories	Protein	Carbohydrates
Sour	1 cup	485	7	10
Whipped Topping	1 cup	155	2	6
Related Products:				
Cocoa	1 cup	245	10	27
Malted Milk	1 cup	245	11	28
Baked Custard	1 cup	305	14	29
Ice Cream	1 cup	255	6	28
Ice Milk	1 cup	200	6	29
Yogurt	1 cup	150	7	12
Meat, Poultry, Fish				
Meat:				
Bacon	2 slices	90	5	1
Ground Beef (lean)	3 oz.	185	23	0
Roast Beef	3 oz.	165	25	0
Corned Beef	3 oz.	185	22	0
Dried Beef	2 oz.	115	19	0
Beef Potpie	1 pie	210	15	0
Chili con Carne	1 cup	560	43	0
Beef Heart	3 oz.	160	1	0
Steak	2 oz.	115	0	0
Lamb Chop	4 oz.	400	0	0
Lamb Roast	3 oz.	285	0	0
Beef Liver	2 oz.	130	3	0
Baked Ham	3 oz.	245	0	0
Boiled Ham	2 oz.	135	0	0
Pork Chop	3.5 oz.	260	0	0
Pork Roast	3 oz.	310	0	0
Frankfurter	1 frank	170	1	0
Pork Links	2 links	125	trace	
Veal Cutlet	3 oz.	185	0	0
Veal Roast	3 oz.	230	0	0
Salami	1 oz.	130	trace	0
Bologna	2 slices	80	trace	0
Braunschweiger	2 slices	65	trace	0

		Calories	Protein	Carbohydrates
Deviled Ham	1 tbsp.	45	0	0
Vienna Sausages	1 sausage	40	trace	0
Poultry:				
Chicken Breast	3.3 oz	155	1	0
Chicken Drumstick	2.1 oz.	90	trace	0
Chicken Potpie	1 pie	535	42	0
Fish:				
Breaded Fish Sticks	10 sticks	400	15	0
Breaded Haddock	3 oz.	140	5	0
Breaded Perch	3 oz.	195	6	0
Sardines	3 oz.	175	0	0
Shrimp	3 oz.	100	1	0
Tuna	3 oz.	170	0	0
Clams	3 oz.	65	2	0
Crabmeat	3 oz.	85	1	0
Oysters	1 cup	160	8	0
Salmon	3 oz.	120	0	0
Eggs:				
Cooked	1 egg	80	trace	0
Scrambled	1 egg	110	1	0
Fats, Oils:				
Butter	½ cup	810	1	1
Whipped Butter	½ cup	540	1	trace
Lard	1 cup	1,850	0	0
Vegetable Fat	1 cup	1,770	0	0
Margarine	½ cup	815	1	1
Whipped Margarine	½ cup	545	1	trace
Corn Oil	1 cup	1,945	0	0
Cottonseed Oil	1 cup	1,945	0	0
Olive Oil	1 cup	1,945	0	0
Peanut Oil	1 cup	1,945	0	0
Safflower Oil	1 cup	1,945	0	0
Soybean Oil	1 cup	1,945	0	0

(Continued)

PROTEIN GUIDE (*Continued*)

		Calories	Protein	Carbohydrates
Creamy Blue				
Cheese Dressing	1 tbsp.	65	trace	0
French Dressing	1 tbsp.	65	trace	3
Mayonnaise	1 tbsp.	100	trace	trace
Thousand Island Dressing	1 tbsp.	80	trace	3
Sugars, Sweets				
Chocolate Icing	1 cup	1,035	9	185
Coconut Icing	1 cup	605	3	124
Fudge Icing	1 cup	830	7	183
Caramel Candy	1 oz.	115	1	22
Milk Chocolate Candy	1 oz.	145	2	16
Chocolate-Coated Peanuts	1 oz.	160	5	11
Mints, Candy Corn	1 oz.	105	trace	25
Plain Fudge	1 oz.	115	1	21
Gum Drops	1 oz.	100	trace	25
Hard Candy	1 oz.	110	0	28
Marshmallows	1 oz.	90	1	23
Chocolate Syrup	1 oz.	90	1	24
Chocolate Fudge Syrup	1 oz.	125	2	20
Honey	1 tbsp.	65	trace	17
Jellies	1 tbsp.	50	trace	13
Molasses	1 tbsp.	50	0	13
Brown Sugar	1 cup	820	0	212
Granulated Sugar	1 cup	770	0	199
Powdered Sugar	1 cup	460	0	119
Pancake Syrup	1 tbsp.	60	0	15
Vegetables				
Mashed Potatoes	1 cup	185	4	24
Potato Chips	10 chips	115	1	10
Radishes	4 radishes	5	trace	1
Spinach	1 cup	40	5	6
Sweet Potatoes	1 potato	155	2	36

		Calories	Protein	Carbohydrates
Candied Sweet Potatoes	1 potato	295	2	60
Tomatoes	1 tomato	40	2	9
Tomato Ketchup	1 cup	290	6	69
Tomato Juice	1 cup	45	2	10
Okra	8 pods	25	2	5
Canned Pumpkin	1 cup	75	2	18
Sauerkraut	1 cup	45	2	9
Summer Squash	1 cup	30	2	7
Turnips	1 cup	35	1	8
Cooked Parsnips	1 cup	100	2	23
Fruits				
Apples	1 apple	70	trace	18
Applesauce	1 cup	230	1	61
Apricots	3 apricots	55	1	14
Apricots in Syrup	1 cup	220	2	57
Avocados	1 avocado	370	5	13
Bananas	1 banana	100	1	26
Cantaloupes	½ melon	60	1	14
Canned Cherries	1 cup	105	2	26
Cranberry Juice	1 cup	165	trace	42
Cranberry Sauce	1 cup	405	trace	104
Dates	1 cup	490	4	130
Fruit Cocktail	1 cup	195	1	50
Grapefruit	½ grapefruit	45	1	12
Grapefruit Juice	1 cup	165	1	42
Grapes	1 cup	65	1	15
Grape Juice	1 cup	165	1	42
Lemon Juice	1 cup	60	1	20
Lime Juice	1 cup	65	1	22
Orange and Grapefruit Juice	1 cup	110	1	26
Prune Juice	1 cup	200	1	49
Oranges	1 orange	65	1	16
Orange Juice	1 cup	120	2	28

(Continued)

PROTEIN GUIDE (*Continued*)

		Calories	Protein	Carbohydrates
Peaches	1 peach	35	1	10
Peaches in Syrup	1 cup	200	1	52
Pears	1 pear	100	1	25
Pears in Syrup	1 cup	195	1	50
Pineapple	1 cup	75	1	19
Pineapple in Syrup	1 cup	195	1	50
Plums	1 plum	25	trace	7
Plums in Syrup	1 cup	205	1	53
Raspberries	1 cup	70	1	17
Raspberries, frozen	10 oz.	275	2	70
Strawberries	1 cup	55	1	13
Strawberries, frozen	10 oz.	310	1	79
Watermelon	1 wedge	115	2	27
Blueberries	1 cup	85	1	21
Dried Figs	1 fig	60	1	15
Lemonade	1 cup	110	trace	28
Limeade	1 cup	100	trace	27
Raisins	1 cup	480	4	128
Rhubarb	1 cup	385	1	98
Tangerines	1 tangerine	40	1	10
Papayas	1 cup	70	1	18
Grain Products				
Bagels	1 bagel	165	6	28
Barley	1 cup	700	16	158
Biscuits	1 biscuit	90	2	15
Bread Crumbs	1 cup	390	13	73
Farina	1 cup	105	3	22
French Bread	1 loaf	1,315	41	251
Italian Bread	1 loaf	1,250	41	256
Rye Bread	1 loaf	1,100	41	236
Pumpernickel Bread	1 loaf	1,115	41	241
White Bread	1 loaf	1,245	41	228
Whole Wheat Bread	1 loaf	1,095	41	224

		Calories	Protein	Carbohydrates
Devil's Food Cake (w. chocolate icing)	1 cake	3,755	49	645
White Cake (w. chocolate icing)	1 cake	4,000	45	716
Yellow Cake (w. chocolate icing)	1 cake	4,390	51	727
Sponge Cake	1 cake	2,345	60	427
Gingerbread Cake	1 cake	1,575	18	291
Fruitcake	1 cake	1,720	22	271
Pound Cake	1 cake	2,430	29	242
Brownies	1 brownie	85	1	13
Choc. Chip Cookies	1 cookie	50	1	6
Sandwich Cookies (vanilla)	1 cookie	50	1	7
Sandwich Cookies (chocolate)	1 cookie	50	1	7
Fig Bars	1 cookie	50	1	11
Corn Flakes	1 cup	100	2	21
Cornmeal	1 cup	435	11	90
Corn Muffins	1 muffin	125	3	19
Puffed Corn	1 cup	115	1	27
Shredded Corn	1 cup	100	2	22
Graham Crackers	4 crackers	110	2	21
Saltine Crackers	4 crackers	50	1	8
Danish Pastry, plain	12 oz.	1,435	25	155
Plain Doughnut	1 doughnut	125	1	16
Macaroni	1 cup	155	5	32
Macaroni and Cheese	1 cup	430	17	40
Muffins	1 muffin	120	3	17
Egg Noodles	1 cup	200	7	37
Puffed Oats	1 cup	100	3	19
Oatmeal	1 cup	130	5	23
Pancakes	1 pancake	60	2	9
Apple Pie	4-inch wedge	350	3	51

(Continued)

PROTEIN GUIDE (*Continued*)

		Calories	Protein	Carbohydrates
Cherry Pie	4-inch wedge	350	4	52
Pecan Pie	4-inch wedge	490	6	60
Pumpkin Pie	4-inch wedge	275	5	32
Cheese Pizza	5½-inch wedge	185	7	27
Popcorn	1 cup	40	1	5
Dutch Pretzels	1 pretzel	60	2	12
Thin Pretzels	1 pretzel	25	2	5
Pretzel Sticks	5 sticks	10	trace	2
Cooked White Rice	1 cup	225	4	50
Instant White Rice	1 cup	180	4	40
Puffed Rice	1 cup	60	1	13
Cloverleaf Rolls	1 roll	120	3	20
Frankfurter or Hamburger Roll	1 roll	120	3	21
Hard Roll	1 roll	155	5	30
Rye Wafers	2 wafers	45	2	10
Spaghetti	1 cup	155	5	32
Spaghetti with Meatballs	1 cup	330	19	39
Waffles	1 waffle	205	7	27
Puffed Wheat	1 cup	55	2	12
Wheat Flakes	1 cup	105	3	24
Shredded Wheat	1 biscuit	90	2	20
Wheat Flour	1 cup	400	16	85
All-Purpose Flour (sifted)	1 cup	420	12	88
All-Purpose Flour (unsifted)	1 cup	455	13	95
Cake Flour (sifted)	1 cup	350	7	76
Self-Rising Flour	1 cup	440	12	93

REST AND RELAXATION

Getting a good workout is important to your everyday health, but proper rest and relaxation is important to your sanity. A heavy workout will break those muscle fibers and put life into your body, but you need recuperation before you can enjoy it. Constantly tearing your muscles will eventually leave you with a skeleton, unless you give your body a chance to heal.

After a tough day of lifting weight, it is hard for your body to relax. Your system is all keyed up and ready for more. Now comes the hard part—trying to get your body to rest so you can recuperate from your workout. If you do not rest, you can never expect your body to operate at its fullest.

When you go to try your maximum attempt, your system will be full of anticipation and adrenalin. After you have completed your big lifts, you will feel relieved and also exhausted. Now is the time to sit down and rest so your body will be ready for your next workout. If you have to, force yourself to rest so you will be ready for future tries. You have to give your body time to heal.

When your body is overworked, it will reject heavy weight. The idea is to keep your system as fresh as possible. You want to learn how to master your relaxation periods, so when you go on your cycle, you can make the best gains possible. If you have to, practice your resting. This way, you will be good at it when your body needs to rest.

Some general signs of an overworked system are: throbbing muscles, a feeling of fatigue, and a shortage of breath. It is important not to mislead yourself into believing that you are overworked every time you feel fatigue. Do not fall into the habit of missing workouts by using the excuse that it is for your own good. Fatigue can come from other things beside a lack of rest, so watch for your mood swings.

The best form of relaxation is sleep. When you sleep, your body has a chance to repair itself with little interruption. Each person's sleep requirements vary with their activity level and body metabolism. For a long time, I could function only on 6 hours of sleep, but eventually I switched to 7 hours per night.

Too much sleep tends to leave me in a dazed and confused state. My body seems to burn off too much nervous energy. If I make a habit of oversleeping, my lifts tend to actually go down instead of up. Too little sleep leaves me feel sluggish and unprepared to physically and psychologically handle big weights. I suggest you experiment with different levels of slumber. Find the correct amount of sleep that fits you and stick to it. Try not to break training, unless it is absolutely necessary.

I feel that the perfect time to train is right after you wake up and digest a big breakfast. That is when your strength should be at its strongest level. Your body should be well rested, and your system should be fueled with a nutritious morning meal. I realize a lot of people cannot train at this time of the day, but everyone should try to use their schedules to allow them to train when they are at their freshest.

Sleep is but one aspect of rest and relaxation. Being able to keep your system running quietly and smoothly is just as important as sleep. A person who chatters constantly or always taps his foot or drums his fingers is wasting precious energy. This energy could be used to replenish the body and build strong muscle tissue.

I suggest that you find a hobby or a positive habit so you can rest and recline after a tough workout. Some lifters use meditation or self-hypnosis; other use the television or the radio as a form of relaxation. The idea is to find something you like to do and relax. When I feel wound up, I like to go out to a movie and have supper with my wife. I also like having a good conversation with friends while sipping a beer, soda pop, or chocolate malt. These are the ways in which I relax, and they work for me. I hope you can establish a positive resting program, so you too can take advantage of all your strength.

Start to monitor your habits and find the things that work for you. Learning how to relax can be fun, so start today. Remember, you have to be well rested before you can fully test your strength.

Spotting for Safety

Safety should be your number-one priority in any form of weight lifting. A new high in the squat is important, but your life outside of the gym should matter more. I never sacrifice safety for anything or anyone. I just don't believe that an injury is worth the risk of bad spotting or poor judgment in order to make a lift. I think since you spend so many hours in the gym improving your health that you should not do anything to jeopardize it.

I will focus my discussion on spotting on the squat because I feel this lift, if done with incompetent spotters, is the most dangerous. If you miss a squat, there is only one way to go . . . and that is down. You should always use three spotters during any squat. One man should stand on each side of the bar and the other should stand behind you ready to grab you if you start to fall or recline.

Spotters should never be afraid to grab the bar or react in any positive way. An alert spotter can justify any move they make. The important thing is that they are alert to any danger. I won't let a person spot for me unless they want to. Forcing somebody to watch over your safety when they do not want to or know how to is foolish. Pick your spotters carefully.

When you spot, you should never position your body in the downward path of the bar. Many times, I have seen a spotter being so overprotective that they have their thigh or knee too far under the bar. The obvious problem with this is the destruction of your leg if the weight falls unexpectedly. Always keep your hands out and your body safely away. With your hands out, you can grab an errant bar safely. Also, with your hands out, you can quickly react to any situation. A spotter who just stands there and watches should sit themselves in the audience.

Give the lifter a chance to make the lift, but be ready in case if they don't. If a person starts to stall and the bar stops on the way up, do not panic. As long as you stay alert, there is no danger. If you think that there is a need to grab the bar, do so, but do it in unison with the other spotters. If you tilt your end, it could be the straw that breaks the camel's back.

With helping a lifter rack the bar after a successful attempt, do it with gentle force. I like a spotter who is assertive in their spotting. After a lifter completes a big squat, they are usually winded and close to the breakdown point. They want to get the weight racked and off their back as quickly as possible. The spotters should guide them into the rack with determination. I don't like spotters who just stand there and let me fumble my way toward safety.

If you expect good spotting, then I suggest you spot good. I have found that people will watch you closer if they feel you are watching over them with the same intensity. I always try to spot my best, and I expect nothing less from the lifters than aid me in my attempts at increased poundages.

Like anything else, it takes practice to be a good spotter. Experience is your best teacher. The important thing is that you can earnestly apply yourself to the pursuit of perfect spotting. As long as you stay alert and try your best, you will always be recognized as a good spotter.

Training Partners

It is hard to accomplish anything in life by yourself. Nearly everything you know you have been taught by someone at one time or another. The true champion can put all of life's lessons together and win. The true champion will also acknowledge the people who helped him on his climb to the top. Life is not a solo walk through time; life is a series of experiences that will lead you to your destiny.

All powerlifters need a coach. They need someone who has been there and can show them the way to success. That is why you are reading this book. It is entirely up to you on which school of thought you will follow, but you will need capable lifters to bring you along. Whether you choose to lift in a group or with a certain individual is up to you. The trick is to find a system from which you can learn.

The problem with relying on a group of lifters is there are too many things you cannot control. Each individual lifter will bring his own personality and philosophy to the gym. At times, this is healthy, but most of the time it will breed chaos. Gym time is too precious to waste on personalities, so if you choose to work in a group, make sure it is a cohesive group.

The ideal situation is to find one lifter you can identify with, and then to work out with other pairs of powerlifters. This way, you only have to concern yourself with one person, instead of trying to monitor a mass of lifters. This one lifter can get your suit and see to your needs, and the rest of the pairs can be there as insurance.

Your powerlifting partner should fit your personality. If you are an optimistic person, you should not link yourself to a constantly depressed, pessimistic lifter. This relationship might work, but it will produce much tension before any advantages will be seen. You do not have to like your partners, but you do have to respect them. Whether you associate with your helper outside the gym is not the question. The question is: can you build a "STRONG" relationship while you are in the gym?

Needless to say, you and your partner should agree on a lifting schedule and a power program. It is a good idea to find a person who is at least as strong as you are. A weaker training partner can give you enthusiasm, but you might need a person who is stronger than you to give you confidence. The ideal situation is to find a lifter in the next weight class and try to catch their lifts. If you could be a mediocre lifter in the 181 class and weigh 165, you would be an excellent 165-pound contender.

A training partner should help you reach your goals. If you lift with a jealous or a selfish person, your career could hit a stall point quickly. If your lifting is suffering, it could be because of the people you work with are not motivating you or are holding you back. Do not hesitate to switch partners. Variety is the spice of life and essential to develop your full potential in a demanding sport such as powerlifting.

I have gone through at least a hundred training partners in my decades of powerlifting. From most of them, I have come away from with good gains and a better understanding of the sport. Some of them left me drained, but the majority left me far better for having trained with them. I try to constantly perfect my style and routine. Fresh training partners bring new experiences and a different point of view to my workout.

I do not advise powerlifting contenders to mix sexes. Men and women both have unique goals and different ways of reaching them. A woman can identify with maximum output, but she cannot identify with 800 pounds squats and really heavy benches. Likewise, men cannot relate as well to a female powerlifter's dreams and goals like another female can.

The main thing is to constantly strive to better yourself. Keep yourself surrounded by top-quality lifters and one day soon, you will be one . . .

INJURIES AND REHABILITATIONS

The most common powerlifting injuries are lower back sprains and muscle tears. They are often the complaints you hear voiced in most gyms. Just because they are common does not mean that they cannot be avoided. You can avoid any injury by taking precautions before it happens.

I have had muscle tears in every part of my body. I have ripped fibers from my toes to my neck. Just recently, I reinjured my shoulder for the umpteenth time. Every time I aggravate my shoulder, my bench falls 200 pounds. I then have to start working it back up again. It starts to get sad when I have to go through and try to make bench presses that I had originally made back in the early 1960s, but that is the penalty for an injury.

The key to rehabilitation is rest. You have to let the muscle recuperate. It is crazy to expect to go through your entire workout with a wrenched back. You have to compensate some of your schedule for the rest required to gain your full power back. I do not advocate skipped workouts, but I do stress caution. I am not telling you to stop your powerlifting career and go to Florida for a month, but I am telling you not to lift too much when your body can't.

I do a lot of recuperative exercises while I am injured. I work other parts of the body until I feel the hurt body part can accept stress. I then apply as little pressure as possible and work up from there. Even when I am injured, I still try to keep the body shocked so it can continue to grow and not deteriorate before my eyes.

When a part of me is hurt, I will overload it with high repetition sets (very, very light weight). I will usually do three sets of 10 reps and build from there. The high reps force blood through the muscle and keep it flushed and more responsive to repair.

I also apply plenty of analgesic balm. This will also heat the muscle and keep it in a constant relaxed condition. With the high reps and moist heat, the injured area will often feel better. Your body will not experience most of the pain that comes with tears and sprains; thus, it can start on the road to recovery.

Never try to put too much pressure on the tender zone until you honestly feel you are ready for it. Trying to come back too soon may aggravate the injury and give way to calcium deposits. Read the messages sent out by your body. If the vibes are right, then by all means start pumping, but don't set yourself up for a psychological block by coming back before your body is ready.

Do not worry about your lifts going down. If you are getting plenty of rest, mild exercise, and using moist heat, your lifts will come back quickly when you are healed. Most of the reductions will be due to mental blocks. Your mind may convince your body that because it was hurt, it should not be strong. I advise you to fight these negative thoughts. If you let a minor injury stop your powerlifting career for life, then I would say "your dream was not strong enough."

You can easily avoid injuries by simply following my TEN COMMAND-MENTS! Knowing your weaknesses is just as important as knowing your strong points. If you know that you are vulnerable to injury due to cold drafts or excessive sweating, then avoid them during your workouts. Try never to severely alter your workout environment. Any changes in your powerlifting habits should be gradual, so your mind and body can adjust to them before any serious problems arise.

Your health and safety should always be your first priority. Before you lift, make sure your area is clear of unnecessarily objects and obstructions. Move all the curl balls and dumbbells to the other side of the room. In my gym, the powerlifting area is separated from other parts of the gym. This assures the lifters that they only have to worry about powerlifting equipment.

Always test your footing before you attempt any lift. If the floor is slippery, you should know before you start your workout. Finding such things out during a workout can be hazardous to your health. Before you squat, test to see how sturdy the racks are and how safe the floor is. If you take the time to do it now, you might be saving yourself from an injury later.

I have seen more injuries occur while lifters were warming up than while they were attempting heavy loads. That is why I stress the need to do your first set slowly. Give your body a chance to communicate with your brain. Just do not grab a weight and start pumping. You might find yourself saddled with an injury you could have avoided. When you first touch the bar, treat it as though it were heavy.

Make your movements slow and cautious and as you get warm and build your confidence, speed it up.

The secret to avoiding excessive pain in powerlifting is: "Practice the basics." If you can master the little things, you can rest assured that chances of injuries will be few and far between. It is usually the minor things that go wrong and lead to major disasters. Try to remember that in order to try for a new max, you have to make it through the rest of your workout safely.

I try to impress upon all my lifters the need to fight through an injury. I'm not telling you to head for the platform in pain, but I'm suggesting that you constantly try to ready yourself for your eventual return. You can spend your injured days being disgusted with your injury or you can fight against your pain and make a speedy return. You might say, "Ernie, what can I do to fight this condition?" My reply is to use what I have outlined in this section.

Do not take much time off, but rest enough so you are ready to start on the road to recovery. Once you feel up to it, start to slowly come back by using light weights to work your hurt areas. You might be able to do heavy sets of certain exercises, but it all depends on where and what kind of injury you have. Before and after your workout, apply plenty of moist heat. If you do these simple things, you can avoid much pain and frustration.

Mistakes in any sports have to be accepted as a part of the game, but in powerlifting, an injury could mean the end of the game. I advise you to watch every move you make in the gym. Don't try to do any foolish thing. The idea is to use your gym time as the means for improving your body, not as a method on inflicting pain upon yourself. An injury is a serious mistake a lifter should avoid at all costs.

Another way to avoid injuries is to start your powerlifting career with a good healthy stance. Many people start out deadlifting with all back and do fairly well at it, but eventually, the pain will catch up to them. An inferior stance can bring you plenty of gains, but in the end, it could bring you to the end of your powerlifting career. If you start out deadlifting 400 pounds with all back, that might seem great to you then, but what happens when you hit that 500 mark, and then the 500-pound barrier?

Eventually, your poor deadlift stance will lead you straight to your injury. It will be very hard to avoid an injury when you are using the wrong muscles to complete the exercise. Look at your stance; ask yourself if it hurts in any way. If the answer is yes, you might need to change your positioning. If you are a novice lifter, start your career by using the stances I outlined in the beginning of this book. Older lifters might want to also try these new stances. The main thing is to lift in a position that will not bring pain, now or in the future.

Some of you are probably looking for a list of exercises you can perform while sidelined with certain injuries. Well, I do not have such a list because I believe in powerlifting and powerlifting only. If you were a wrestler, you would not play hop-scotch to get back into your career; likewise, a powerlifter should not go outside of his field on order to start his comeback.

I advocate the use of stretches and light powerlifting movements. Stretches will warm you up for a more vigorous attack on your muscles. Light weights will supply the needed pressure to again promote physical growth. By using only (or a lot of) powerlifting movements, you will not only keep your stance perfected, but you will already be on your way back.

A person who injures his back should take time off so he can be physically prepared to return. Then he should proceed to start out slowly to do light deadlifts. If you were to avoid deadlifts and do bent rows or shrugs, you might set yourself up for a mental block when you choose again to start to deadlift. You can do all the shrugs you want to, but in the end, you will have to deadlift or else admit defeat and end your powerlifting career. But do not worry if you use the Frantz Rocker because then, you should never have to worry about a bad back.

When I tear my shoulder muscle and my bench drops 200 pounds, I use the bench to bring it back up. I could spend my days doing dumbbell presses or files, but instead, I choose to return immediately to powerlifting. I do not want to give my mind a chance to negatively affect the performance of my body, so I get right back on the horse that threw me. I will start out with many light sets, but the second I feel that I am ready, the weights start to climb.

Your attitude can affect the time it takes to recuperate from an injury. If you "think" an injury means the end of your career, it just might. You have to keep a positive attitude and work toward success. You just cannot lie down and accept a setback—you have to want to fight through it and salvage your lifting career. If I had let injury stand in my way, I would not be standing here today. How long it takes you to return to the platform depends on how badly you want to.

While you are allowing your body to heal from an accident, let your mind continue to grow. Mentally go through some of your past workouts. Remind yourself of the reasons why you want to get stronger and return to the sport. Read articles, magazines, and books on the sport you love so much. Keep your enthusiasm up by loading your brain with powerlifting thoughts. You will be surprised at how these "strong thoughts" aid in your recovery.

Most important, use this sidelined time to review your workout routines and schedule. This intense look at your progress may help to spot your weak points in your routine and help you to get through an injury while avoiding future tragedies. You can even start to plot a plan of action to use once you are strong enough to resume lifting.

The important thing is to mentally and physically fight an injury. If you use one part of your being without the other, you might prolong your layoff. You have to put all your energy into successfully coming back. It will be a tough fight, but one, I assure you, that is worth taking. The end result will be lifelong mental and physical health.

Another reason why you have to mentally fight an injury is because you have to keep your mind in tune with your body's reactions. You cannot allow yourself to get mentally blocked out of any lift. If you want to return to the sport, you have to think hard about your recovery. By putting a great deal of mental juices into your lifts and by coming back through the use of light powerlifting movements, you should be able to avoid the unwanted mental jinx.

One more thing, you have to be on guard for is—FEAR. Once you make your successful return, you have to make sure you are not afraid to pour on the heavy weights. Likewise, this can be a problem with lifters who have never been injured, but are afraid that they might be. You must remember "carelessness causes most accidents." Follow the principles I have already told you about and the ones you will learn soon. Commit this whole book to memory and the chances of you being injured are slim.

Powerlifting should be a safe sport, and it can be if you apply some thought before you act. If you don't prepare to step onto the platform, you can expect the worst, but if you think about what you are about to do, you should do it fairly well. The idea is to increase your power, not to hurt your body, so be careful and watch yourself grow.

WOMEN'S POWERLIFTING

In the old days, men were powerful figures and women were their obedient partners. The man was the one who shouldered the heavy burden. Times have changed; men are no longer the dominant factor. In fact, I guess you can say women are getting stronger these days in both spirit and body.

Women's powerlifting became a reality just a short time ago. It was not until the 1980s that women's strength training was recognized as a constructive and productive activity. Since then, women have made the sport a real spectacle. Women hold their own tournaments and crown their own champions. They are slowly turning the sport of strong men into a family affair.

My wife is one of the reasons why women's powerlifting progressed. Diane Frantz has consistently shown the world that women can compete in a once male-dominated sport. Diane has made some truly amazing gains in an activity few people thought women could stand up in.

Diane has held or holds close to 50 National and World records. She holds the women's 123 pound records and most of the 132 pounds records. Diane coasted to an easy victory in the 1984 Women's Nationals. She took the title in the 132-pound class by coasting to an easy 1,000-plus total and finishing ahead of the second-place winner by over 100 pounds.

My wife started powerlifting in the 1970s. At first, I thought that it was her way of getting more of my attention, but then I saw how serious she was toward her training. Before I knew it, Diane had attracted other women to our health studio. These women were not there to body build; they wanted to work the Big Three.

The Ernie and Diane Frantz Health Studio soon became a focal point for women's powerlifting. I still had my championship men's team, but now, all of the sudden, I had the makings of a good women's team as well. It was like starting my coaching career over again. I had to familiarize myself with a whole new world—the world of women's powerlifting.

Since the 1970s, I have trained several female World Champions. I have used the same techniques to train them as I have used with men. The only variation is a higher concentration on the squat and the deadlift. I do not believe women were made to be good benchers.

I support women powerlifters as long as they keep their femininity. I do not respect a woman who tries to be like a man. It is one thing to try to better yourself; it is another thing to try to be somebody else. Some women act more masculine than most men. I cannot admire a woman who tries to act like a man just to gain attention or a little recognition. The sexes were made to be different, and I think that powerlifting should keep them that way.

There is nothing wrong with a woman trying to better herself, and I like to see girls trying to improve their bodies and confidence through weight training. I never thought I could appreciate a strong woman until my wife started her powerlifting career. Now, I cannot picture our relationship without weights. Powerlifting has been a big thing in my life, and now it is a big thing in ours. Only time will tell how strong our relationship can grow.

Diane and I are the "World's Strongest Couple." I finished second in the 1983 Nationals (by 5 pounds), my wife finished first in the 1984 Nationals. This means that we were the strongest married couple in all the land. We are very pleased with this distinction, and we work hard to live up to the label. We planned to increase our hold on this image by having a great day at the 1985 Nationals.

It's amazing, but some of the lighter women can even match male totals, but as the body weight goes up, the male physique takes over. A woman's structure just cannot pack on the muscle like a man's, and for that, most men are thankful.

In my opinion, women are just as competitive as men are. They tend to get more emotional about their efforts. They seem to realize that they have to make gains and break stereotypes all at the same time. Men already have records to shoot for and totals to beat. Women are just starting to lay the foundation for future female powerlifters.

I was named as one of two coaches to the 1984 Women's National team competing at the World's. I was very happy to receive this honor. I hope I can grow with this exciting new sport. I included a women's division in all my powerlifting meets. I feel they deserve much recognition, and I am trying my best to give them as much as I possibly can.

The women at my gym worked very hard for their powerlifting successes. All of them surprise even themselves with their initial strength gains. You cannot accuse any of the girls at the Frantz Club of not trying their hardest. In fact, sometimes, I feel they try too hard. That sounds hard to believe coming from a man like me, but these women do amaze me. Sometimes, when my wife was pulling in the deadlift, I will wince in pain.

When it comes to my wife and the rest of the girls, I have to remind myself of the basics of powerlifting. The old slogan goes "no strain, no gain," but sometimes I wish it would not apply to females. Then I see their success, and I realize that the agony I suffer does not compare to the positive thing that powerlifting brings them. I forget that my wife feels the same way I do when I am lifting a heavy load. When a person is not under the weight, they tend to imagine pain the actual lifter does not feel.

The future of women's powerlifting is an extremely bright one filled with lots of promise. Every day more and more women realize the rewards that strength training can bring them, and many of them are accepting the challenge and trying to better themselves. Future women will never have to worry about being victimized by a male, but men might have to reevaluate their social standing.

Two women that I am really proud of are examples of females expanding their lives through weights. One is Felecia Johnson; the other is Maris Anne Sternberg. Felecia is a lightweight who is quickly reaching "superstar status." She is just a little thin, but she lifts big weights. Maris is my heavyweight champion and also Diane's best friend. Maris has had a lot of success under my coaching and finished second on last year's Women's World's.

Both of these women have worked very hard to reach their levels of success and neither of them have yet fully reached their powerlifting peak. You will be hearing more from Felecia and Maris as their workouts mount in intensity and they fully master their weight careers. Confidence is more important to women because they have no idea of their true potential. A woman gains confidence through experience, but she also has to be constantly reminded of her past successes. When I work with my women's team, I exercise caution thorough my instructions.

Many people think that female powerlifters are big, chunky, abnormal girls. Like I said before, a woman's body structure does not allow her to get too massive. A girl has to spend a lot of time straining before she gets bulky muscles. She also has to eat a lot and sleep more. Weights will simply tone most of the muscles on the female body. The lady will still be soft, but she will be firm as well. The only time a woman will get masculine through weights is if she lets and wants it to happen.

Most movie stars that pawn their ideas about muscle shaping have no idea what lifelong muscle conditioning is all about. A girl needs to put pressure on her limbs the same as a boy. The only way to successfully improve the quality of your body is to force it to grow. There are no shortcuts to a healthy life. A woman has to exert herself before she can see real changes in her figure. Diane Frantz will soon come out with a complete book on female powerlifting. Until then, I urge women to use my thoughts in this book . . . and to be careful.

COMMON COMPLAINTS

There are a few complaints that are common in powerlifting. I hope to answer some of your questions in the following paragraphs. The reason some of these questions are sometimes stated as complaints is because the lifter lacks adequate knowledge to label them otherwise. After this section, you should be able to identify and correct any popular problems of powerlifting. I have broken down the subject matter into three parts. They are: sore joints, stretch marks, and a constant feeling of fatigue.

SORE JOINTS

Whenever you start a new activity, you are going to experience stiffness. This comes about because the muscle is not used to being worked from that angle. You are using your muscles in a motion that at first is foreign to your system, and at the same time, you are applying a great deal of increased pressure. These two combined produce sore joints.

An easy way to avoid this problem is by warming up the muscle before you use it. You can do this by using light weights to prepare your body for the shock of your heavy lifts. It sounds so easy, and yet, many lifters still refuse to take the time to warm up. Most of them know the consequences and still will not spare the time needed to save their joints.

Equipment can also help relieve sore joints. A strong suit or a pair of knee wraps can give the body an elastic feeling that will help you flow through your squats with little or no jerking action. Equipment will physically and mentally prepare your body for the pressure of the weight.

I occasionally take cod liver oil tablets to lubricate my joints and prevent stiff-ness and/or soreness. The tablets tend to make my joints function as if they were freshly oiled. If you take the tablets, warm up properly and use your equipment wisely. You should have no problems with your joints. Also, make sure you avoid snappy movements that could put pressure on the wrong muscles. Your body is a reflection of your training routine.

STRETCH MARKS

These ugly red lines occur when the body grows faster than the skin can expand. If you put muscle on quickly, you will force your skin to explode outward. This is a de-sired goal because it will give you that big physique most lifters strive for. What you do not need is stretch marks. They hurt a physique by giving it a butchered look.

You can avoid stretch marks by lubricating the skin from the inside out. If you are taking cod liver oil tablets, your system is already receiving inside lubrication. Now, all you have to do is apply an outside shield. I take vitamin E because it's closest to the natural oil of the skin. This vitamin will keep your skin supple and ready to expand without stretch marks.

If you already have these crude trademarks, I still urge you to use this infor-mation. It might help to ease your current marks and prevent new ones from ever starting.

CONSTANT FEELING OF FATIGUE

Fatigue can result from a number of things: lack of motivation, too much sleep, negative mental framework, or just stale workout habits. Fatigue is probably the number-one criticism of powerlifting that most ex-lifters state as their reason for retirement.

A person has to occasionally remotivate himself/herself into the world of pow-erlifting. This can be done by simply changing your workout habits. You can change your stance, alter your reps, work new angles, or change your workout partner; all of these can add new life to your lifting. By constantly changing your powerlifting pattern, you can add a whole new dimension to your workout. This fresh feeling will lead to new gains and a healthier outlook.

I motivate myself by entering new competitions. I use a meet as an instru-ment to measure my progress. When I feel I am bored with my training, I enter a powerlifting meet and start a new cycle. If I have to keep trying for a new total, I know that I have to avoid the powerlifter's rut.

Sometimes we forget what originally made us powerlift. We forget what made us so enthused with the sport from the start. It helps to sit down and recollect these old feelings, and then to apply them to our current lifting. Write your thoughts about powerlifting down on paper and keep them around so you can read them when you need a boost.

If you constantly try to better yourself and "THINK" through your workouts, you will never get bored with lifting. Fatigue comes when you stop growing, and as long as you memorize this book, you will never stop progressing. You can never get tired of striving to improve yourself . . . unless you lose sight of your goal. Fight fatigue by being prepared to handle those poundages.

POWERLIFTING MYTHS

Powerlifting has been labeled with a few undeserved characteristics. These labels have been handed down from one misinformed generation to another. I have no idea when and where these fictions were originally uttered, but I do know that they should stop spreading now. This is the time to set the record straight and once and for all stop the spread of certain rumors.

Stereotypes can be found for every type of sport you can name. This does not mean that they are true statements; it simply means that people who know nothing about an activity have seen fit to pass judgment on it. Powerlifters have not escaped some cheap labels. These labels not only disrespect current powerlifters, but discourage future champions from entering the sport. I would like to shed some light on a few of these dark areas.

POWERLIFTERS ARE DUMB

For the life of me, I cannot figure out why this rumor even started. It could be that people were intimidated by strong men, so they labeled them as undesirables and, thus, unworthy of the usual communication most people give each other. This would explain why some people who have never met a strongman already have a preconceived notion about his intelligence.

If a novice to the sport of powerlifting took time out to talk to a few of the more experienced lifters, he would realize just how much intelligence is needed to become a successful lifter. A master powerlifter has to regulate not only his workouts, but his food intake, sleep, and all other parts of his training. It takes a person with some degree of intelligence to monitor all of these things at once.

105

Most of the world's biggest brains lift or advocate lifting weights as the fastest form of muscular development. You can spend years trying to stimulate your muscles to grow by using calisthenics or hours getting a good workout with weights. Most smart individuals would choose spending hours to build muscle tissue through the pumping of iron. I don't understand how such people can be labeled dumb.

Weight lifters have made a decision to improve their bodies. This group of people has decided to devote some of their lives to the pursuit of physical perfection. How can we label such people as dumb, when they have made a decision that will enrich their entire lives? It's the people who let their lives and bodies deteriorate who should have their intelligence checked.

Your soul and spirit should be housed in a frame that can carry them proudly. The body should be treated as a temple. The body you have now will be yours forever; the only choice you have is how it shall look. I like to work and groom my body because I feel that it helps my mind relax and thus, promotes mental health. It takes an enormous amount of concentration to successfully lift heavier and heavier poundages. In order to concentrate, you must control your thoughts and emotions. I feel it takes brains to control your brain.

You must have some intelligence in order to use the knowledge you gain through experience. If a lifter is dumb, he will not benefit from his mistakes; thus, he will spend forever doing them. Experience is a valuable tool if you are equipped to handle the information you learn. As a lifter, you have to analyze your training and decide what is best for you. The only way to make gains is to think about them.

Powerlifting is getting more and more scientific. Lifters are using all kinds of data to determine when their peak periods are. It is no longer a sport where a human being is defenseless against an iron element. Nowadays, powerlifters are armed with strategy, but they must understand themselves and the world around them before they can profit from any type of serious training.

MUSCLE TURNS TO FAT

Some people are under the impression that if you stop pumping iron, or if you grow old, your muscles will turn to fat. This is an absurd statement! How could fat be thought of as an old muscle? It makes no sense to consider the two as related in any manner.

To say that muscles turn into fat is to say that plastic turns into glass. Of course, we realize that neither comparison is factual. You develop muscles in the process of tearing down and rebuilding body tissue. Fat comes about through a surplus of calories ingested to calories used. If I lift a heavy weight, it will tax my system and exhaust my muscles. If I allow these torn muscle fibers to heal, they will mend stronger than they originally were. This will produce strong muscles.

If I were to eat a cherry pie, and then go to sleep, I could promote fat because my system would not be utilizing these calories. If every time I eat more calories than I expend, I will develop fat deposits. This fat will lie on my body until I work it off by cutting my calories and/or increasing my physical output.

How can anyone assume that muscle can turn into fat? One comes about through work, and the other comes about with no work. It is impossible to get fat through muscle tissue. How this rumor ever started is a real mystery, and one we will probably never solve.

If a person develops a good physique through weight lifting, and then stops lifting, he might lose some size. The amount of his loss will depend on the type of muscle gained and the activity level of the ex-lifter. If the muscle gained was a quality tissue gained through powerlifting, and if he maintains some form of vigorous exercise, his physique might only contract slightly. Muscle gained through quick repetitions with light weights will disappear quicker. This is mainly a blood pump and should go away when the muscle is not continually pumped with blood.

If you have a lot of fat, you can turn it into a muscle. This is not a magical process. What you do is use your excess calories (fat) to fuel your body during your workouts. Eventually, your fat will be replaced by quality muscle tissue. There is nothing mysterious about this because your change in appearance will be due to your hard work.

When a weight lifter stops working out, he should revise his menu. A mistake most lifters make is forgetting to limit their calorie intake after reducing their exercise levels. If you stop your workouts and do not replace them with an equally draining activity, you will have a surplus of calories to burn. If you do not burn these calories, you will develop fat deposits. Your muscles will still be there; they will just be hidden behind the fat.

POWERLIFTERS ARE MUSCLE-BOUND

Some people think that powerlifters are muscle-bound. They believe that we are creatures that are doomed to a life of restricted movement. They think we cannot run or enjoy activities that take coordination or agility. This is another stereotype that should have been stopped immediately after it started. The amount of agility is different with every lifter. Some men do a lot of other exercises to promote flexibility; others just practice the Big Three and accept the lack of movement as a price to pay for power. Auxiliary exercises tend to drain the body and hamper muscular growth. How much flexibility each lifter possesses is up to that particular lifter.

Lifting heavy weights will limit your flexibility because the muscle will get thicker and used to working at a certain angle. If you squat a lot, your legs will be used to going up and down with a lot of pressure. You cannot expect these same legs to run a marathon. Running uses different muscles and requires more endurance than squatting does.

You can limit your loss of flexibility through the use of agile sports, but as I stated before, you will be burning off calories you could be using for muscle recuperation. The choice is up to you. Whether you value the increased size or flexibility will determine what you choose to do. Most powerlifters do not think it is worth the trouble of all that extra sweat just to have a little more flexibility.

I use table tennis as a means for keeping my reflexes sharp. If I am not in a cycle, I will play table tennis as often as possible, but once I am headed for new heights, I cut down on all unnecessary movements. Table tennis does the job for me. I find it keeps me limber and provides a needed break from my powerlifting routine, but again, I will not play if I am on my cycle. When it is time to do some serious powerlifting, I only powerlift.

I hope this generation will be the one to pass on factual information to future powerlifters. The days of stereotypes and lies are over. People are finally looking into the sport that has been wrongly labeled for so long. We are finally getting the respect we have worked hard for.

Powerlifting is a sport that takes brains and brawn. One without the other will hurt you in your quest to be a champion. I urge you to powerlift, but I urge you to do it from all sides. Sure, get in there and strain, but more important, learn about the sport that can change your entire life.

Powerlifting is my "Fountain of Youth." It keeps me young. Every day presents a new challenge to meet and conquer. I learn something new about myself during every workout. I am constantly learning what makes me tick and how to use this information to better my daily life.

There are many powerlifting fictions, but the fact is the sport is good for you. I hope all of you readers will work toward cleaning up stereotypes whenever you hear them. You can make a difference, if only you stand up and let yourself be heard. Powerlifting is an intelligent activity for intelligent people, so be proud. We are just at the beginning of what promises to be a glorious powerlifting history.

OFFICIAL RULES FOR THE BIG THREE

You can have all the strength in the world and still not win if you do not know the rules. A person who is skilled in the legal requirements for a lift has a big advantage over the lifter who is not prepared. Rules are a part of life. They serve to structure our activity and help in determining a winner. You can easily be one of the winners if you follow the words in this book and learn the rules of powerlifting. I suggest you spend some time learning the official rules in the World Powerlifting Federation and International Powerlifting Federation.

SQUAT

The lifter must have their suit up, and they must face the front of the platform. After taking the bar from the racks, the lifter must move backward to establish his position (Note: these rules vary by federation and if a monolift is used). You must assume an upright position with the top of the bar not more than 3 cm below the top of the anterior deltoids. The bar should lie across the shoulders in the horizontal position. Your hands should grip the bar, and your feet must be flat on the floor (no wedge at the heel or toes can be used). You must not hold the collars, sleeves, or the plates at any time during the performance of the lift. However, the side of either hand may contact the inside of the inner collars.

Once the lifter is in the proper position and motionless, the referee shall give the signal to squat by using a downward motion of the hand and the word "squat." Once the signal has been given, the lifter shall bend the knees and lower the body until the surface of the legs at the hip joint is lower than the tops of the knees.

The lifter shall then recover at will, without double bouncing, to an upright position. Once the knees are locked and the lifter is motionless, the referee will make a hand motion and use the word "rack." The lifter must make a real attempt to rack the bar. If you miss the lift due to a spotter's error, the judges can grant you a new attempt.

CAUSES FOR DISQUALIFICATION OF THE SQUAT

During the lift, failure to wait for the referee's signals.

Any change of the position of the hands on the bar.

More than one recovery attempt or double bouncing.

Failure to assume an upright position at the start and completion of the lift.

Failure to bend the knees and lower the body until the surface of the legs at the hip joint is lower than the tops of the knees.

Any shifting of the feet during the performance of the lift.

Any shifting of the bar or the body during the performance of the lift.

Any touching of the bar by the spotters before the referee's signal.

Any touching of the legs with elbows or upper arms.

Failure to make a bona fide attempt to return the bar to the rack.

BENCH PRESS

The lifter must assure the following position on the bench, which must be held during the lift: the head and trunk (including buttocks) must be on the bench at all times; hand spacing shall not exceed 81 cm as measured between the forefingers, and the lifter's shoes must be flat on the floor (varies by federation). You may ask one or more spotters to help you get the weight at arm's length. The referee's signal shall be given when the bar is absolutely motionless at the chest. After the "CLAP," the bar is pressed vertically to straight arm's length and held motionless until the referee says "RACK."

CAUSES FOR DISQUALIFICATION OF THE BENCH PRESS

During the uplifting, any change of the elected lifting position.

Any raising or shifting of the lifter's head, shoulders, buttocks, or legs from the bench, or movement of the feet.

Any heaving or bouncing of the bar from the chest.

Allowing the bar to sink excessively after the referee's signal.

Any uneven extension of the arms.

Stopping of the bar during the pressing part.

Any touching of the bar by the spotters before the referee's signal to replace the bar. In this case, the referee may award a new lift due to spotter's interference.

Failure to wait for the referee's signal.

Touching against the uprights of the bench with the feet.

Touching the shoulders against the uprights of the bench.

Allowing the bar to touch the uprights of the bench during the lift.

DEADLIFT

The lifter must face the front of the platform. The bar must be laid horizontally in front of the lifter's feet, gripped with an optional grip with both hands, and uplifted with one continuous motion until the lifter is standing erect. At the completion of the lift, the knees must be locked and the shoulders thrust back. The referee's signal shall indicate the time when the bar is held motionless in the apparent finishing position. Any raising of the bar or any deliberate attempt to do so shall count as an attempt.

CAUSES FOR DISQUALIFICATION OF THE DEADLIFT

Any stopping of the bar before it reaches the final position.

Failure to stand erect.

Failure to lock the knees.

Supporting the bar on thighs.

Any shifting of the feet during the performance of the lift.

Lowering the bar before the referee's signal to do so.

Allowing the bar to return to the platform without maintaining control with both hands.

Note: Review the rules of your federation prior to your training cycle for competition as there are raw, equipped, command and disqualification variations between federations.

POWERLIFTING NOW
AND IN THE FUTURE

Powerlifting, as we know it today, has only been around since 1968. Before that, there were a lot of strong men, but they had no universally accepted means for testing their strength. The muscular man has always been a showcase. One of the best features of any circus or sideshow is the strongman: the human being who pits his strength against the element of iron.

The powerlifter used to be stereotyped as a dumb, muscle-bound freak of nature. People used to gawk at his unnatural talent. In the old days, if you even mentioned that you lifted weights, people would classify you as a weirdo or a loner. Most of society knew little about the sport we spent our lives practicing.

Nowadays, everybody lifts weights. Boxers, tennis players, runners, etc., use iron as a form of training. Football players, wrestlers, etc., use weights as a source of power. Every sport today will pump iron for various reasons. The main two reasons are power and endurance, but weights can be used to achieve any goal. What was once an activity practiced by a selected individuals is now a common practice performed by every athlete. Even the layman who does not indulge in other sports pumps iron.

Weight lifting is now the number-one form of body conditioning. If you want to better your physique, you could spend years doing calisthenics or hours lifting weight. Most people have chosen to lift iron, because it is not only convenient, but fun as well.

Some people lift weights to satisfy their ego; others do it to protect themselves. A small minority does it to make money, and a large majority does it to feel good about themselves. Whatever the reason is, the main thing is that these people are trying to better themselves.

I feel it is every man's dream to be a superhuman. Look at our fascination with such characters as Superman and Spiderman. These are superhuman fantasies that possess amazing power. I often sit in front of the television and wonder what the world would be like if everyone could be faster than a speeding bullet, more powerful than a locomotive, and able to leap tall buildings in a single bound.

In a world where everyone is confident in their abilities, there would be no need for violence. People could relate to each other on the same level. We would not have to worry about some coward using a weapon while our backs were turned. Everybody would have faith in their neighbor because they would have something in common; they would be trying to honestly better themselves.

People who test their physical limitations are often people who go through life testing themselves. They are the kind of people who set goals for themselves, and then strive to meet them. I think violence comes with insecurity. When you are not sure about yourself and your abilities, you tend to strike out at life. Wouldn't it be great if everyone practiced some form for physical exertion?

Powerlifters often respect each other for different reasons than do other groups of people. We respect each other because we know the sacrifice and pain we had to endure to reach the top of our sport. When I look at another champion, I know what he had to suffer to get where he or she is today, because I had to go through the same type of program.

Some people are under the impression that all you have to do is to take steroids and you will be a strongman. I cannot begin to tell you how wrong that statement is. Steroids cause the body to repair itself faster than normal. This allows for quicker muscular gains. Steroids do not work the muscles; they do not tear the muscle tissue. You, as a lifter, have to apply the work required to break down muscle tissue. This so-called wonder drug does not get you new heights. You have to lift the weight that brings you glory. The lifter has to supply the guts needed to lift heavy poundages. Wouldn't it be great if all we had to do was to take steroids and we could lift tons of weight? No! Why would we want to get something for nothing? There would be no pride in going out to the platform and popping a pill for strength.

The challenge comes from going to the platform alone, armed with only knowledge and good training. That is the real test in life. I am proud of every moment I have spent struggling with a new max. The thrill comes from bettering yourself, and do not let anyone tell you differently. If you were given your victories on a silver platter, they would have no meaning, but when you work for them, they mean everything.

People in sports get all conceited. There are some powerlifters who have swollen heads and matching egos. You cannot avoid getting braggers in any form of physical exercise. It would be nice if people did their thing and did not have to throw it in other people's faces, but some do not, and we just have to live with that.

I do not think people should brag about themselves in an unproductive manner. Constantly ranting and raving about your strong points to teammates will eventually get you no teammates. As Emerson once said, "Do not tell me who you are—what you are speaks so loud, I cannot hear you." Truer words have never been spoken, and I hope you see the wisdom in them.

It is stupid to walk around telling people what you can do when they can see you do it. Just because a person benches more than the next guy does not make him a better man. Let us face it: If we were rated by our words, at times, all of us would be guilty of an occasional boast. The thing I want to stress is that all men are different. Just because some powerlifters represent themselves in one way does not mean we are all that way.

The powerlifting personality that you display is a product of your upbringing and your lifting environment. If you were brought up as a talker and not a doer, then you will talk a good game. Likewise, if you lift in an area where men are constantly boasting to assert their masculinity, then you will be more likely to boast with them. How you were raised and where you live will determine how you will act in the gym.

I think as a person gets power, he also gets confidence and thus, becomes a humble man. When a person knows or tests his physical limitations, he also knows what he is capable of exerting as an individual. This knowledge tends to give him confidence in himself and both, toward his lifting and toward life. This feeling of confidence can allow a person to sit back and enjoy life instead of trying to fight it.

It is a known fact that a little confidence goes a long way. A person who sets goals and tries to better himself is a person who can let his actions speak for itself. It is the person who doesn't try to do anything with his life that the society should watch.

Today, the sport of powerlifting is booming. Every day, more and more people are introduced to this exciting way of life. The number of lifters has continued to multiply. Our sport continues to gain the recognition it deserves.

Every country in the world has a powerlifting team. We complete against each other in such events as the World Cup. The sad fact is we are not an Olympic sport. Olympic lifting consists of overhead presses. I used to be an Olympic-style lifter way back in 1953. I enjoy that sport, but I do not find it as exciting and stimulating as powerlifting.

We currently have our own National Championships. The winners from each weight class represent our country in the World against winners from the same class in other countries. The only problem is, though our supporters grow with each event, we will do not get the universal coverage that the Olympics do. I am sure most of us would like to represent the United States in a competition that all Americans can watch and be proud of.

Back in 1968, when I first started to sponsor competitions, I had to spend much of my own money to do it. I felt it was important to upgrade our contest, so I started to run legal meets that followed the specifications set down by the reigning powerlifting association (AAU).

Nowadays, a meet is a lucrative business. The number of lifters more than covers the cost of the production. I get much satisfaction out of bringing together a group of lifters and letting them show their skills. I am proud of the fact that I have supplied the means for so many lifters to reach their dreams.

Spectators are even increasing with the times. It is not uncommon to see 5,000 people at a national event. Granted, that it is not as many people compared with a baseball or football crowd, but you have to consider your limited media attention. If more people were exposed to our sport, then more people would want to get involved.

Times are getting better. More and more people are being drawn to our sport. Television is slowly starting to take an active role in our development. The future of powerlifting is an extremely bright one. Hopefully we can gain full-scale recognition by the end of the decade. I do not mean partial acceptance by a minority of people; I mean *full* acceptance by the majority of humans on this planet.

I encourage everybody to try powerlifting. It could be the most rewarding thing you will ever experience. Do not be afraid of failing. A person can only lose when he/she does not try. Set some goals for yourself and strive to meet them. Everyone should join the powerlifting generation.

THE FRANTZ
HEALTH STUDIO

We opened the Ernie and Diane Frantz Health Studio in 1962. We felt there was a real need for a gym where people could get good sound advice at reasonable rates. Our studio caters to this need. We had roughly 250 key members; most of them show up on an occasional basis; others practically live in the gym.

The gym was originally a floor-rented operation, but times had been good to us. We owned the whole building. Three floors were filled with every type of equipment made to build a good physique. We had all kinds of machines and plenty of free weights. Our gym was also equipped with a sauna and a Jacuzzi bath.

I probably had the cheapest rates in all America. To join our studio, all you had to pay is $250 for the year. Then, as an extra inducement to continue your membership, I cut the fee in half for the second year. Your first visit will cost you nothing but your time. Everyone is invited to come in and work out.

I operated a weight lifting store from within the gym. There, you can buy all the essentials. I stock everything from vitamins to clothes, but the three things I am proudest of are my suits, wraps, and protein. These are the instruments I have used to build my power career.

My specially designed powerlifting suit and wraps were a product of years of experience and experimentation. They were the outcome of decades in the sport.

My protein was designed to give you maximum energy. It was a special blend that I recommend to any serious lifter. we had the best and biggest powerlifting and bodybuilding team in all America. Our teams are still universally recognized, and I spend a great many hours with them. Anybody could join these teams. All it takes is a desire to be the best you can be.

BLAISE BOSCACCY (1984)

Ernie: Name some of the weight lifting titles you hold.

Blaise: I have won the State and Junior National Championships. I also won the YMCA Nationals.

Ernie: When did you first get involved in powerlifting?

Blaise: I started lifting back in 1973, but I did not seriously give power a try until January 1981. Now, I'm into powerlifting so much that nothing can stray me from my goal.

Ernie: How did your lifting relationship start?

Blaise: I remember those days clearly. We used to blitz the bench on Saturdays at the old gym. We would spend hours working that lift. I think that is where I developed my passion for the bench.

Ernie: What kind of coach am I?

Blaise: You have always struck me as a very positive instructor and with 3 decades of experience, you represent a real gold mine of information.

Ernie: What is the most important thing I have taught you?

Blaise: You have taught me to keep pushing when things get rough; but more important, you have shown me not to let an injury stop my training.

Ernie: How much weight have you gained during your lifting career?

Blaise: I was always a big boy, so when I started lifting, I already weighed a healthy 215 pounds. My current weight is 325 pounds of packed-on muscle.

Ernie: How old are you, and does age matter in powerlifting?

Blaise: I am 28 years old, and you are a living proof that age has nothing to do with power. When I get your age, I hope I can still handle the big poundages.

Ernie: When did you know that powerlifting was your sport?

Blaise: After my first meet I knew that I was hooked on power. There was something about being out on that platform that turned me on.

Ernie: Is weight lifting your number-one priority?

Blaise: My family comes first, but weight lifting is a close second. I feel lifting helps me to be a better family man, by allowing me to feel good about myself and by allowing me to work toward positive goals.

Ernie: What are some of your goals?

Blaise: I have only one big goal, and that is to be a World Champion. I am aiming for the top, and I am not planning on anything to stop me. I want to be the best, and I am training for it now.

Ernie: How would you like to be remembered in powerlifting?

Blaise: I would like to be remembered as a strongman who always took the time to work with others.

Ernie: What kind of advice would you give to a novice lifter?

Blaise: Always be consistent in any phase of powerlifting. Never skip workouts or intentionally hurt your power career.

Ernie: What has powerlifting taught you about yourself?

Blaise: Powerlifting has developed the competitive side of me and has taught me how to handle some of my moods. I think that I know myself better because of lifting.

Ernie: What season do you experience your best gains in?

Blaise: The spring and the fall are always the high points of my cycle. I think it is because the weather is mild, and my body feels and performs better.

Ernie: What makes the Frantz Team the best around?

Blaise: We get along and are not afraid to help each other. A lot of teams are hampered by jealousy among their members. At your gym, we grow together and enjoy ourselves along the way.

Ernie: Do you body build?

Blaise: No! I do not want to waste my strength.

Ernie: Are you a big eater or sleeper?

Blaise: Both.

Ernie: Have you ever had an injury?

Blaise: In the past, I have; pulled a muscle in my chest, wrench my lower back, and twisted a knee. Thanks to you, I have fought during these setbacks.

Ernie: What kind of education do you have?

Blaise: I have a junior college degree.

Ernie: What is your biggest victory?

Blaise: I have not had it yet, but with your help, I will in the future.

BILL NICHOLS (1984)

Ernie: What are some of the contests you have won?

Bill: I am somewhat of a rookie in the sport, but in the short time I have competed, I have won numerous state and local contests. I have yet to win a major contest in my own eyes, because my goals are so high.

Ernie: When did you start powerlifting?

Bill: Early in the year in 1981.

Ernie: When did our lifting relationship start?

Bill: On April 11, 1983, when I first walked in the gym to see who I could train with. You pulled me aside and started talking, and before I knew it, I was a member of Frantz Power Team.

Ernie: What kind of coach am I?

Bill: You have been a big influence on my power career. In early 1983, my best total was 1,875 pounds; in 1 year, with the help of you and your team, my total is now just under 2,100 pounds. I think that this says it all.

Ernie: What is the most important thing I have taught you?

Bill: To listen and learn from those who are willing to share their knowledge.

Ernie: How has your body weight changed?

Bill: It has gone from 200 to its present 250 pounds.

Ernie: What is your favorite lift?

Bill: The total that is what wins contests. I enjoy the squat, and I'm a good bencher, but the results are what make me happy.

Ernie: What else do you do for fun?

Bill: I body build when I get bored. I like to work the major muscle sections. I don't go crazy with shoulder work or other smaller muscles, but I do like to pump the big muscles.

Ernie: What is your biggest victory?

Bill: My biggest victory is not a physical one, but a mental one. I have realized in the year that I have been training with you that someday I will be a Senior National Champ and a World Champion. This insight has made me eager to train, and so I have been pushing myself more.

Ernie: How would you like to be remembered as a powerlifter?

Bill: As a champion.

Ernie: What kind of advice would you give to a novice lifter?

Bill: To use their head and always listen and train hard.

Ernie: What has powerlifting taught you about yourself?

Bill: If you put your mind to something and truly believe in yourself and concentrate, a person can do anything they want to. Powerlifting has taught me that anything is possible if a person is willing to work hard.

Ernie: How old are you?

Bill: I started lifting in my early 20s; I am now 26 years old. I hope when I reach your age, I can have a big total and be the man to beat for powerlifting trophies.

Ernie: What season do you experience your best gains in?

Bill: Right now, every season is a good one. My total continues to climb under your direction, and at this rate, it probably will continue to grow for a while yet. I can't at this point pick a season—all I can do is to be thankful I'm having steady success.

Ernie: What is the best gain you ever made in a lift in 1 day?

Bill: I put 40 pounds on my squat in 1 afternoon. Needless to say, it was a very good afternoon.

Ernie: Have you ever had an injury?

Bill: I have cracked several ribs, dislocated a shoulder, pulled my back, and have had sciatic nerve problems, but none of these setbacks has stopped my powerlifting career. I think that it's important to keep pushing on even when times get rough.

Ernie: Have you ever gone into a lifting rut?

Bill: Yes, a couple of times I have been stagnant for a little longer than necessary, but this usually happens because I overtrain. Sometimes I forget that there are limits to how much weight the body can handle.

Ernie: What kind of education do you have?

Bill: I have my bachelor's degree in political science and forensics.

Ernie: What is your occupation?

Bill: I am a police officer in Naperville, Illinois. Sometimes my powerlifting helps me in my job; other times, I get razzed by my friends as being a real "Supercop," but I wouldn't change my strength or my job for anything.

Ernie: If you had one wish, what would it be?

Bill: To be a World Champion is my big dream, and I plan to spend the rest of my life working toward it. I think powerlifting is the key to success, and I plan to practice until I master it.

FRANCIS RUDY RUETTIGER (1984)

Ernie: List some of your biggest victories?

Rudy: I am a "five-time" State Champion of Illinois, 1980 Jr. National Champ, 1982 National Cup Champ, and just last year I won the YMCA National.

Ernie: When did you get involved in weight lifting?

Rudy: In 1972 I ran into Jim Pumphrey, who is an Olympic lifter, and he introduced me to both sports. I didn't really get into powerlifting until I entered my first contest. I won it and have been powerlifting ever since.

Ernie: How did our lifting relationship start?

Rudy: Our relationship was sparked at a powerlifting meet in 1975. I was told by some friends that you were a World Champion and a great trainer, so I walked up to you and introduced myself. You acted like we were old friends for years and offered to help me in my powerlifting.

Ernie: What kind of trainer am I?

Rudy: The best. You seem to be able to identify a lifter's strong and weak points. You really know how to get the most out of a man's abilities.

Ernie: What is the most important thing I have taught you?

Rudy: Discipline and self-confidence are the two biggest things I have learned from you. These two things helped me in other parts of my life.

Ernie: How has your body weight been affected by weight training?

Rudy: My weight has steadily gone from 126 pounds to my current 160. I desired to be heavier so I could keep stepping up a weight class as I got stronger.

Ernie: Is weight lifting your number-one priority?

Rudy: Yes!

Ernie: Is it hard to be a competitive powerlifter?

Rudy: Yes, at times it's very difficult, because in order to be successful you have to work at it all year-round.

Ernie: What is your biggest victory?

Rudy: The 1980 Jr. National Championship was my first big victory, and it established me as a real contender for World recognition, so I would have to say that that so far is my biggest victory.

Ernie: How do your friends react to your feats of strength?

Rudy: They are very supportive, and they always tell me how impressed they are. I try to let them know that it's nothing unusual. Anyone can do it, if they invest their time and energies.

Ernie: What are some of your goals?

Rudy: I plan to win the Sr. Nationals, and then I want to reach my dream, World Champion.

Ernie: How would you like to be remembered in the history of powerlifting?

Rudy: I would like to be remembered as a nice guy who never quit when the going got rough. I would also like to be remembered as one of the best lifters in my class.

Ernie: How old are you?

Rudy: I was 19 when I became a serious powerlifter, and I am 30 years old now.

Ernie: What makes the Frantz Power Team work?

Rudy: The person who owns the team and the people he has put together.

Ernie: Do you body build?

Rudy: Only in the off-season, when I know it can't hurt my powerlifts. I would never think of competing in a bodybuilding contest.

Ernie: Are you a heavy eater or sleeper?

Rudy: I'm a heavy eater, but a light sleeper.

Ernie: Have you ever had an injury?

Rudy: No! I have been very cautious and a little lucky; so thankfully, I have avoided the injury problem.

Ernie: Have you ever gone into a lifting rut?

Rudy: Yes, I had one rut that lasted an entire year.

Ernie: What is your occupation?

Rudy: I'm a machinist at Caterpillar, and I also work as a strength coach.

Ernie: If you had one wish, what would that be?

Rudy: To be a World Champion.

MARIS ANNE STERNBERG (1984)

Ernie: When did you first start powerlifting, and what are some of your wins?

Maris: I began my career in April 1980. Since then, I have been the State Champion 5 years in a row. I have also won the Regionals and the National Cup. In 1983, I was the U.S. Nationals Champion and a silver medalist at the World Meet.

Ernie: How did our relationship start?

Maris: You approached me at a meet in Lafayette, Indiana, and told me that I was not using all my potential. You then gave me an open invitation to train in your gym.

Ernie: What is the most important thing I have taught you?

Maris: You have taught me consistency, good form, and how to have humility as an athlete.

Ernie: When you were growing up, did you ever think you would be a powerlifter?

Maris: Absolutely not!

Ernie: How much do you weigh?

Maris: When I started lifting, I weighed 185 pounds; I now train at 212 pounds of body weight.

Ernie: When did you know that powerlifting was your sport?

Maris: When I first felt the squat bar on my back, I knew I was doing something I had a future in.

Ernie: What else do you do for fun?

Maris: I play the violin, needlepoint, and practice my photography. Just because I powerlift does not mean that I play football or enjoy other rough activities.

Ernie: What is your biggest victory?

Maris: That would be a toss between my medal at the Worlds and my 501-pound squat.

Ernie: How do your friends react to your feats of strength?

Maris: Sometimes they think I'm crazy, but on the whole, they seem to take it pretty much in stride. Of course, I don't push the issue either. If the subject comes up, I discuss it, but I do not make a point of rubbing it in.

Ernie: How far do you think you can go?

Maris: I believe I have the potential to be the best there is.

Ernie: What kind of advice would you give a novice lifter?

Maris: Keep a good form, practice consistently, and find a good coach. A good coach can make all the difference in the world. I've seen you give your competition some really crucial pointers; that's why I think an unselfish coach is a necessity.

Ernie: How old are you?

Maris: I started lifting late in life. I was 32 before I touched a weight; I will be 36 in September.

Ernie: What do you think of male/female powerlifting?

Maris: In your gym, everyone works together with a minimum of problems. However, I do not agree that women and men should compete against each other. As far as knowledge and experience goes, I most certainly believe that men and women can be equal, but in strength, men have a big physical advantage.

Ernie: What season do you experience your biggest gains in?

Maris: My best lifting seems to occur from March through June.

Ernie: What makes the Frantz Team the best around?

Maris: The Frantz Team is a very unique bunch of people. They are a very close, friendly group; but they are not cliquish. The team is very quick when it comes to accepting a new person into the group. They are also a very dedicated group of lifters and take their craft very seriously. You can tell when we travel around to various meets, people always respect us and seek us out.

Ernie: Do you body build?

Maris: Only to the extent that I need to help my powerlifting. One of the reasons I started power was because I found bodybuilding boring.

Ernie: Have you ever had an injury?

Maris: Yes, but not from lifting; I had back surgery in 1976.

Ernie: What kind of education do you have?

Maris: I have a B.A. in music ed. and an M.A. in special ed.

Ernie: What do you do for a living?

Maris: I taught school for 9 years. Currently, my husband and I have a music store located in Downers Grove, Illinois.

Ernie: If you had one wish, what would that be?

Maris: I think my one wish would have to be for financial security. If I had that, I feel that it would free my mind to be able to devote myself totally to my lifting. Often, problems will be there in the back of my mind during workouts (business, bills, etc.) that I would rather be rid of. I pretty much have everything I want. I am very happy with my life right now, and a major reason is the fact that I have been able to improve my body and my self-image through my powerlifting.

THE FRANTZ FAMILY IN 1984

By: Diane Frantz

For my husband's fiftieth birthday, I gave him the best present I could think of. It was my victory in the 1984 Women's World Powerlifting Championship, and I have been working toward this gift for over 5 years. The date was May 19, 1984, and the place was Santa Monica, California. Fred Hatfield sponsored this year's event and nine different countries competed for powerlifting honors.

I got the chance to represent the United States by winning the National competition sponsored back in January by Chip McCain. The Nationals were held in Austin, Texas, and they were really fun for me. I took the title in the 132-pound class by a margin of over 100 pounds. My World victory was a bit tougher because the judging was extremely critical. A lot of the lifters bombed out because of squats and benches that were almost perfect.

I was fortunate to get my openers in before any mistakes had a chance to occur. As it was, I only squatted 385 pounds, benched 181 pounds, and deadlifted 407 pounds for a total of 973. This was far behind my high marks and way below my average working out, but due to the high level of pressure and the close judging, I felt lucky to have posted that total.

I was happy to win such a big contest on Ernie's birthday. He was real proud of me and coached me every second of the way. I do not know what I would have done if Ernie had not been on that platform with me. Yet again, it would have been a hollow victory if Ernie would not have been there to share it with it. My husband is the reason why I became a powerlifter, and I am a product of this experience.

Five years ago, I decided to try the sport that Ernie had grown to love. My husband let me train after-hours in the backroom until I had enough form to start lifting out of the rack with experienced lifters. When I first started, I knew I wanted to go to the top where Ernie was. I wanted to feel what he felt and see powerlifting through his eyes. Powerlifting gave our marriage a bond that other married people spend a lifetime looking for.

I had a naturally strong deadlift, but poor form in the squat. Ernie would make me start every workout with the squat. I would do set after set, and rep after rep. We would train in the morning before he went to work in the prison and after our children had gone to work or school. Ernie would coach me for an hour or two while handling other lifters or some minor business transactions.

I was 40 years old before I even thought about powerlifting, and I am now 46 and at the happiest time of my life. My husband was so patient with me, and everybody at the club helped out so much that my World victory was definitely a family win. I am just glad that my dedication to the sport was great enough to be honored with this highest of awards. I hold over 40 American and World records, but they don't measure up to an actual World title.

Needless to say, I will remember Ernie's fiftieth birthday forever, but the important thing is that it was the end of the dream but the beginning of the future. My goal had been reached. When I was 40 and decided to try my luck at powerlifting, I could have chosen a lesser goal, but my pride wouldn't let me. I wanted to be the best, and I was determined that the best I would be. I worked hard for my goal, even though some people thought it was too late in life for me to reach it. They thought time was against me and my own aging body would be my biggest block. I tried to convince them of my sincerity to attain my goal, but their attitude said that I would have to physically show them.

It took 5 years, but I did reach my mark. I hope other people will be influenced by this fact. You do not have to be a spring chicken to try your hand in a new activity. I was over 40, but thanks to Ernie and positive thinking, I was able to invest my time in a productive hobby. I would like to see older people get involved in a new life. The world is changing, and we have to change with it.

Life since Ernie has been absolutely wonderful. Together, we have a lot of terrific children. They are: Dave, 26 years old, Laurie, 25, Dan, 24, Pat, 22, Tom, 21, Gail and Jean, 20, and Ernie Jr., 15. When we all get together, we make a big deal of it because everyone loves everybody so much. The whole family believes in positive thinking because that is the method of thought that Ernie and I have tried to convey. You are what you think, and the examples you set will determine your reality. We try to set good, healthy examples because we believe in good, healthy living.

As you probably gathered, most of the family does lift weights. Tom has taken the sport of bodybuilding as his flame in life. He won the Teenage Mr. America a couple of years ago and is currently training for future contests. He is almost as big as his father, but only time will tell how much success he will have. The sport of bodybuilding can be a rough experience if the participant is not prepared for their scores, but Tom should do well because he trains hard and knows the importance of rest.

The family lifter we are the proudest of is little Ernie. He likes to imitate his father and try all of the basic power moves. He currently trains once a week and has posted totals of 270 in the squat, 110 in the bench, and 275 in the deadlift. It really is a sight to see when Ernie Jr. gets to the gym when Dad is around. Someday, little Ernie will carry on the family tradition. He may never be as physically strong as my husband, but he will definitely have his strength in character.

We are a close-knit family, and I hope we stay that way forever. Honesty is our big rule, and we all try to remember that when dealing with others. This world moves fast, and a person has to be honest with himself before he/she can expect the world to be honest with them. All of us are trying to help out at the gym, and we are constantly trying to make new members feel comfortable.

Some people wonder what will become of me now that I have climbed the mountain. I will still continue to powerlift, but I might only compete in the Master's Division (over 40 years of age). Competing against all those young women is making me an old lady. The pressure is, at times, unbearable, and now that I have reached my goal, I don't really have to deal with it anymore.

I would like to talk Ernie into competing with me in mixed pairs bodybuilding, but he wants to train for one more powerlifting Nationals. I hope to continue to train mornings at the gym and to maybe help other women who are interested in power. My big goal is to plan a strategy that will lead me to the Ms. Olympia bodybuilding title. I would like to see if I could become the best in two worlds. It would be a challenge, and at this point, I am debating whether I really want it.

I advise the world to powerlift because strength training is essential to life. I do not care if you are a man or a woman. If you want to improve yourself, grab a barbell and work. Life is easy when you have a goal and positive people to help you reach it. My family is strong, and I am proud of them.

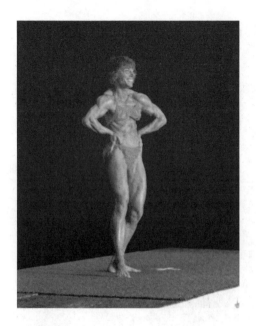
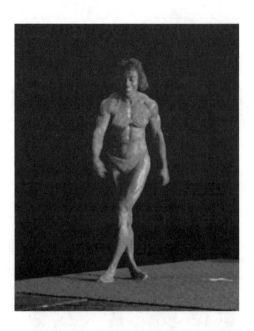

POWERLIFTING GLOSSARY

Amino Acids:	Nitrogen-containing acids that are the building blocks of proteins.
Arch:	Benching posture that allows the chest to expand to its fullest.
Big Three:	The combined name for the squat, bench, and deadlift.
Blood Pump:	Bloated feeling brought about by a lot of fast reps with a light weight.
Bodybuilding:	A sport that judges a person by the quantity and symmetry of their muscle structure.
Bomb:	To drop out of a meet by missing all three of your assigned lifts in one category.
Champion:	A person who has strengthened through the theory of powerlifting.
Clamp:	To clutch the bench with your knees.
Class I Lifter:	A powerlifting total that classifies the lifter as a contender.
Class II Lifter:	A powerlifting total that classifies the lifter as a fairly good lifter.
Class III and IV Lifter:	A powerlifting total that classifies the lifter as a beginner.
Down Set:	Testing a weight by squatting down with it, but getting help to come up.

Elite Lifter:	A powerlifting total that classifies the lifter as a member of the Powerlifting Hall of Fame.
High:	An attempt a little above the parallel in the squat.
In:	Expression used to show good depth in a squat.
In the Hole:	During a contest the lifter who is next to be "on deck" and two lifters away from lifting.
Master Lifter:	A powerlifting total that classifies the lifter as a true champion in the sport.
Max:	Stands for the maximum weight the lifter has successfully done in the past.
Meet:	A contest that enables you to show your strength in the squat, bench, and deadlift by allowing you three tries at each.
Mood Swings:	Your emotional highs and lows.
Novice Lifter:	A lifter who has never won a prize in a powerlifting contest. A novice does not lift directly against an open lifter.
Off-Season:	A period of time when your intensity is reduced.
On Deck:	During a contest the lifter who is due to lift next.
Open Lifter:	A lifter who has won an award for his lifting efforts. Open lifters do not directly compete against novices.
Parallel:	A squat where the bottom of the hips are aligned to the knees. One inch from the pocket.
Peak:	Being at the end of a cycle.
Platform:	The actual lifting area.
Platform Panic:	Being unprepared for a contest.
Pocket:	Imaginary zone in the squat where the bottom of the hips passes the top of the knees. Indicates a good squat.
Powerlifting:	A sport officially founded in the mid-'60s that measures the strength of its participants.
Priority Lift:	A lift that is given extra attention (by working it first in your routine) because it is doing very well or very poorly.
Progress Checker:	A method for tracking your gains over a long period of time. It usually consists of a lifting day or a certain lift.
Protein Supplement:	A powdered form of nourishment that contains all of your essential amino acids.
Pull:	A spoken encouragement for the deadlift.
Push:	A spoken encouragement for the bench.
Rep (Repetition):	One full movement in an exercise.

Rest:	Time to allow worked muscles a chance to recuperate.
Set:	A number of repetitions done together.
Shorts:	Quickly bouncing a weight halfway off your chest.
Single:	One repetition of a weight.
Spotter:	An individual who is there to make sure that the lift is executed properly.
Steroid:	Artificial hormone that enables the body to heal faster and thus, grow stronger quicker.
Straps:	Pieces of material that aid in the grip on the deadlift.
Subtotal:	Your total in a meet when you have already posted your squat and bench.
Suit:	Garment worn to support the body during the lift.
Total:	The amount of your best tries in the squat, bench, and deadlift.
Trophy:	The reward for good training.
Vitamin B2:	A complex growth-promoting vitamin (Riboflavin) found especially in milk and liver.
Vitamin B6:	A compound that is considered essential to vertebrae nutrition.
Vitamin B12:	A complex cobalt-containing compound that occurs especially in the liver and is essential to normal blood function, neutral function, and growth.
Vitamin C:	A vitamin especially from fruits and leafy vegetables that functions chiefly as a cellular enzyme (complex mostly protein product of living cells that induces or speeds other chemical reactions).
Vitamin D:	A vitamin especially from fish liver oil that is essential to normal bone formation.
Vitamin E:	Any of several fat-soluble vitamins that are essential to good nutrition.
Weight Class:	A method of deciding who lifts against whom. Weight classes for men are: 114 pounds, 123, 132, 148, 165, 181, 198, 220, 242, 275, and Super Heavyweights. You must be under a number to compete in the class.
Wrap:	A stretch bandage that strengthens the joint; it is applied to feel more secure and elastic.